WELCOME TO THE
BANGKOK
SLAUGHTERHOUSE

WELCOME TO THE BANGKOK SLAUGHTERHOUSE

The Battle for Human Dignity in Bangkok's Bleakest Slums

Father Joe Maier
Foreword by Jerry Hopkins

PERIPLUS

Published by Periplus Editions (HK) Ltd, with editorial
offices at 130 Joo Seng Road #06-01/03, Singapore 368357.

ISBN 0-7946-0293-2

Printed in Singapore

Distributed by:

North America, Latin America & Europe
Tuttle Publishing
364 Innovation Drive
North Clarendon, VT 05759-9436
Tel: (802) 773 8930; Fax: (802) 773 6993
Email: info@tuttlepublishing.com
www.tuttlepublishing.com

Japan
Tuttle Publishing
Yaekari Building 3F,
5-4-12 Osaki, Shinagawa-ku,
Tokyo 141-0032
Tel: (03) 5437 0171; Fax: (03) 5437 0755
Email: tuttle-sales@gol.com

Asia Pacific
Berkeley Books Pte Ltd
130 Joo Seng Road #06-01/03, Singapore 368357
Tel: (65) 6280 1330; Fax: (65) 6280 6290
Email: inquiries@periplus.com.sg
www.periplus.com

10 09 08 07 06 05
6 5 4 3 2 1

Contents

These are true stories about life in the Klong Toey Slums of Bangkok. Several names, relationships, and minor details have been changed. These stories originally appeared in a slightly different form in the *Bangkok Post.*

FOREWORD

The Rev. Joseph Maier took a seat at the table across from me and as I ordered two mugs of Heineken draft, he took a call on his cell phone. Father Joe, as he's known, is an American Catholic priest who's lived in the Bangkok slums for more than thirty years—despised by some in both low and high places, but loved, and even revered, by more, or at the very least, respected for his spirit and fortitude in his determination to help the poor.

It was January 2, 2000, the start of the new millennium, and we'd met to celebrate numerous past failures and occasional victories, and a future of more of the same. A moment later, he ended his call, abruptly stood, and said, "There's been a gas leak at the ice house. You want to come along?"

We ran to his '96 Toyota Corolla, and just seconds later, as he sped through the Bangkok night, driving as I'd never seen him drive before, he explained his fears—that this ice house was close to his Mercy Centre; and his Mercy Centre, as I already knew well, had homes for the children under his care and an adult AIDS hospice.

"Tell me what you know about Freon," he said. "I don't know much," I replied. "What I remember from a high school science class is that it's an odorless, colorless gas that has no effect on humans, but according to more recent studies, it screws up the ozone layer. Why?"

He said they told him Freon was leaking into his neighborhood, Klong Toey, population 130,000, the largest of some 1,200 urban areas that are officially designated as slums in Bangkok. About a year earlier, Father Joe said, there had been a fire in the same ice house and it should have been shut down back then, but the owner paid a visit to a local politician, who paid a visit to a city inspector, who paid a visit to a fire official and nothing was done. That's the way troubles are handled in Bangkok, and in much of the rest of the world as well.

We were still speeding through the streets, squealing as we hit the corners, bouncing into and out of potholes. I started to laugh.

"What's so funny?"

"I had a thought. You know all those movies where the cop is driving an unmarked car and he gets a call, then reaches out the window and puts one of those flashing lights on the roof? I just had an image of you doing that, except you have a flashing crucifix instead."

He laughed as we slid around another corner and the rest of the way to the factory, we argued about what kind of noise should be coming out of the car when the crucifix was in place.

We agreed it couldn't be a siren or anything that sounded like cops or an ambulance.

I argued for Gregorian chants and Father Joe held out for "Ave Maria."

At our destination, our joking stopped. "That's not Freon. It's ammonia," I said as we exited the car and sniffed the pungent air, "and that could seriously kill somebody."

All around us, street life proceeded as usual. At a food stall across the narrow street from the ice house, people ignored the bad smell and spooned up bowls of noodle soup. How unusual, after all, was an offensive odor in a Bangkok slum?

Father Joe assessed the situation and we took off on a trot towards his Mercy Centre, where once he was assured that everyone inside was out of harm's way, he left me with a friend. Bangkok is one of those unusual cities where personal safety was much assured everywhere and at all times, but Father Joe insisted that unless you were from Klong Toey, you were better off with a local chaperon. As a longtime resident known in the neighborhood, he figured he was exempt from any such threats.

Father Joe traveled the hundred meters or so without me, arriving at the neighborhood police station, out of breath but firm of opinion and resolve. For the next twenty minutes, the portly, balding, sixty-year-old priest from South Dakota, whose mixed Irish and German blood boils at thirty degrees Celsius, the average daily temperature in Bangkok, informed the police who had the misfortune to be on duty that night precisely how they were shirking their duty. Why weren't any cops on the scene at the ice house, he wanted to know. Why weren't they on the community loud speaker announcing the dangers from inhaling ammonia gas? Was anything being done about the leak? Did they even know how harmful ammonia was? What was the plan if someone got sick?

In these situations, cops like to get rid of Father Joe as quickly as possible, even if they have to capitulate a little. So in a short time, it was agreed that the police would dispatch someone to the ice house with one of those battery-operated megaphones and search for any injured or ill, both in the plant and the immediate neighborhood, and if any were found, to take them to the hospital.

Then after collecting me, Father Joe and I hot-footed it back to the ice house, where he confronted the owner, who was sitting nonchalantly on the loading dock—the smell of ammonia still noxious in the air. Now, Father Joe gave him holy hell, causing him to lose a bit of face as there were several others present, but extracting a promise to pay for any possible hospital costs.

With the cops arriving and the owner getting up to greet them, Father Joe and I returned to his car. "This," he said as we walked, "is how journalists and priests get killed."

I laughed again. "Happy New Year to you too, Joe."

[Four people were hospitalized and released in a day or two. The ice house was closed for a week while only the most perfunctory repairs were made to the pipes and gas tanks.]

I met Father Joe eight years earlier, in 1993, at a Christmas party held in his honor and attended by some of the numerous foreign expatriates who served as members of his unofficial support group. On the way, a mutual friend, who invited me to tag along with him, told a story about Father Joe.

As many as 10,000 Southeast Asian children were sold into prostitution each year, my friend said, and Father Joe bought children himself, but in his case, he bought them away from the brothels. One child, about eight, the daughter of a prostitute, was being kept by a brothel, along with other children born to prostitutes, and "raised like pigs on a farm" for future exploitation. Father Joe negotiated a price of US$800 for the child, what the brothel claimed it cost to feed and clothe her for eight years. Now she is enrolled in one of Father Joe's schools and lives in one of the homes in his Mercy Centre, watched over by a mix of Buddhist employees and Catholic nuns and sisters.

At the party, as a journalist who smelled a book or at least a magazine story, I approached the reverend like a heat-seeking missile. The encounter was incandescent.

When I asked him how he ended up in Bangkok, he said he was a product of the Sixties: a priest, yes, but a sort of hippie, too, a Grateful Dead fan, a young man who, forty years later, still hadn't cut the four-letter words from his conversational vocabulary. He said he was among the half-dozen of his fellow seminarians who protested the Vietnam War and the deaths at Kent State University, and lobbied for liberalization of seminary rules. He said that after he and the other mavericks were ordained, the church gave them the most remote and undesirable assignments. Father Joe said he had no interest in going to Thailand, but it was a free trip to the opposite side of the world at an exciting time and he figured that the church would have to bring him back eventually, so he went.

And stayed.

Now—over thirty years later—he is the director of a large aid and self-help organization that has enormous and effective reach among Bangkok's poor. He has kindergartens all over the city, with over 4,000 slum kids enrolled. He also organized several playing fields in the slums and sponsors almost sixty soccer teams for the older kids.

"If the young kids learn how to read and write, they have a chance," he said, "and if the older kids get to put on a uniform and play soccer or volleyball for a season, then they have a chance. If not, by age fourteen or fifteen, they're lost and probably lost for good, and in their case, not for the good of anyone."

We talked about several non-government organizations dedicated to ending child trafficking. I mentioned a few that I suspected were mainly well-meaning amateurs.

"Aren't we all?" Father Joe said.

He went on to explain that the secret of whatever success he experienced was because he always played by the neighborhood rules. I asked for an example. He said, matter-of-factly, "Never steal someone else's heroin." He said he'd tell one story and then had to greet his other guests. The story was about a couple of fifth-graders who found a substantial cache of heroin in one of their school toilets, about a hundred packets. They took it to the principal's office and the principal called Father Joe, who called the police and told them that their job was to roar over there in their police cars, sirens wailing, make a big fuss and search the school, then praise the children in front of the rest of the school and pin medals on their shirts.

"Those were the rules the police are supposed to play by," he said, "and they did." A day later, he went on, a few hoodlums approached these same children and slapped them around a bit. That's a violation of the rules, according to Father Joe. First, they stashed dope in the school and then they intimidated school children. Two rules were broken and in Klong Toey, there's no waiting for Strike Three. Father Joe called the police and told them what happened.

The hoodlums were "politely" asked to leave the neighborhood. Nobody has seen them since.

In the years since we first met, Father Joe and I have become good friends, something I consider a great honor, and no small part of that privilege is to hear Father Joe tell his stories with such empathy about his poor neighbors in the Klong Toey slums. Many of these stories spin the same web that entangles millions of the poor throughout the world and inevitably

make you think of Mother Teresa. In fact, when Father Joe
guided Mother Teresa around the Klong Toey slum in 1971, she
said something quite simple that changed his life. She told him
to stay in the slums, where the need was great.

When I tell people that Father Joe lived in a squatter's shack
with a corrugated metal roof for twenty years, they don't believe
me. For most of that time he slept on a simple cot, clothed himself out of the church box, and led Sunday mass for the residents
of what's called the Slaughterhouse. This is the part of the Klong
Toey slum where for over fifty years, the livestock that fed
Bangkok—cattle, but mostly pigs and water buffalo—were hit
over the heads with metal pipes every night and then sliced and
chopped into parts to be delivered to the city's markets that open
at dawn. Buddhism forbids the killing of any living creature and
Islam avoids all pork, so the butchers were Catholics, many of
them ethnic Vietnamese from several generations back.

Here, between the bustling port on the Chao Phraya River
and the cement abutments of an expressway, thousands of poor
ethnic Thais, Laos, Khmers, Vietnamese and countless illegal
immigrants from Burma live in ramshackle shacks on stilts
over a swamp choked with garbage and unrealized dreams.
Many of them are part of Father Joe's congregation at the
slum's Holy Redeemer Church. Joe is a Redemptorist priest.
What that means, put simply, is that his focus is on redemption,
the act of being set free, or saved. In other words, Father Joe is
an eternal optimist.

In the early nineties, the Port Authority of Thailand, the
government bureaucracy that owns most of the land under the
Klong Toey slum, converted part of the Slaughterhouse into a
parking lot for ten-wheeled trucks. They brought *yaa-baa*, a
methamphetamine, right to the Slaughterhouse door about the
same time that most of the slaughtering was moved to the city's

outskirts. This deprived many Slaughterhouse residents of work and introduced the replacement business: the merchandising of what the Thais call "crazy medicine."

Methamphetamines were not new to the community but this time, they brought with them newfound and ostentatious slum wealth. It was interesting to see those who sold the stuff build new faux stone facades on their shacks and move in modern entertainment sound systems. They had their own enclave in one part of the Slaughterhouse near the new parking lot for trucks—a kind of slum Beverly Hills—until the Port Authority announced that it was bulldozing that area too. There was more profitable use for the property. More parking space for trucks.

By then Father Joe had seen the best and worst that humans can produce, and not all of it in the slums. When Father Joe talks about the "worst," he's probably talking more about various bureaucrats, politicians and law enforcement personnel than he is about his friends and neighbors in the slums, some of whom are pretty well deep into what the church calls sinful activity.

Father Joe's view is that yes, many slum folks bring on their own troubles, but nine-and-a-half times out of ten, slum dwellers are the victims.

The hazards of slum life were numerous to begin with. Then crazy medicine took hold of the slums and raised the level of violence. At the same time, the number of homeless adults and children with AIDS swelled. Also, more migrant children from upcountry provinces ended up on Bangkok streets. After the economic collapse hit Southeast Asia in 1997, things got even worse. Many slum parents could no longer take care of their offspring. Domestic abuse saw a sharp rise in incidence, as did pedophilia, a malignant presence that has grown along with Thailand's notorious sex industry through moral as well as economic poverty.

It wasn't all bad news. Father Joe opened new schools, until there were more than thirty throughout the city's slums. When the building that housed his first AIDS hospice and children's homes was sold and he was given only a month to relocate, a local construction company put 400 men on the job twenty-four hours a day and built an eighteen-bed hospital and street kids shelter in time to meet the bulldozer's deadline, in the least desirable place in the slum, hard by the busy port, where everything floods when it rains.

Today that building is gone, replaced by a new structure built on the generosity of a single brick-and-mortar donor. The new Mercy Centre includes an expanded home for over forty mothers and children with HIV/AIDS, a respite care facility for adults with AIDS who cannot care for themselves, an AIDS homecare and counseling center, four homes for the more than 250 children in the care of the foundation (two others are off-premise), a street child outreach and law center that sees over 100 cases every month, a successful slum women's credit union, a community service center responding to family and neighborhood emergencies, a jobs program for the handicapped, a three-story preschool with 500 neighborhood children in attendance, and what Father Joe is embarrassed to call "the director's facility," a two-storey house in which he now lives—all of this on land the foundation doesn't own, and constructed without approval or permission. Father Joe is a squatter, like those for whom his dreams were built.

Joe laughs when he takes people on a tour. "We're mad," he says. "Barking mad."

Jerry Hopkins
Surin, Thailand 2004

A few notes on Father Joe's stories:

For nearly a decade, Father Joe has been writing stories about his family, friends and neighbors in Klong Toey, often with a harsh realism that shocks the casual reader of the Sunday *Bangkok Post*, where his stories continue to appear sporadically every three or four months to this day. Some stories are about the joys of his slum neighbors' most simple triumphs. Others tell of the extraordinary friendships between orphans, street children and children with HIV/AIDS. All of them speak of the struggles of slum life. The happier ones are truly joyous. The sad ones, many readers have claimed, are among the saddest stories ever told.

They are each extraordinary in their love and sympathy for the poor.

JH

Note: At the time most of the stories were written, one Thai baht equalled about two and one-half US cents.

AUTHOR'S PREFACE
Welcome to the Bangkok Slaughterhouse

We're talking about street crime here: the violent, bloody stuff you can see. Not the uptown kind, like fiscal years and large purchases being timed according to retirement dates.

Unsolved crime is fashionable in the Slaughterhouse, or Rong Mu. The rape of a thirteen-year-old girl a few months back, for example. They haven't found the bad guys. The lost-and-found game is usually based on finance—the financial status of the victim's family or friends vs. the credit rating of the perp.

If the victim's family has a "loud" name, we say, or has money in the bank rather than a simple one-baht-weight gold chain, then the bad guys get found. Otherwise, they usually stay lost. And the unreported crimes. You can't do anything if it's not written down in a day ledger somewhere, and then it all depends on how it's written down in the ledger. Just reporting an incident or filing a complaint means nothing. It has to be in writing, and it's best if the story gets into the newspapers too. But that doesn't happen very often. Crime in the slums? A yawn is a typical response.

Then there is the little stuff—little to the uptown folks and the authorities—the "Three Ks," so called for the KKK brand of rubber cement, which is sold in small green cans. You pour the liquid contents into a sturdy plastic bag and then place the bag over your nose and mouth and breathe deeply. The longtimers don't "track" too well, even in the best of circumstances.

Then there's "Snake," or paint thinner, and the biggest of them all, the "Horse," an amphetamine called *ya ma*, or *yaa-baa*. For someone new to *ya ma*, a quarter of a pill or one *kha*—one "leg"—keeps you bright-eyed and brain-dead for eight to ten hours, and gives the illusion of strength to work more hours, kill more pigs, drive your truck longer, or keep your drinking going without sleep. The real crazies eat eight full pills in twenty-four hours. That way, it only takes four or five weeks to fry your brains.

Here's something else small that nobody pays any attention to: moneylenders slapping around someone late with their debt payment, plus the loud verbal abuse. A moneylender in the slums is all mouth, no ear. No listening to woeful tales of why the poor souls cannot pay.

You don't have protection in the slums. Nowhere to turn. No one to help you. Some say that's how those folks in Italy began a long time ago: providing protection at a cost, but at a lower price than the alternative.

"To ride on the back of the tiger," as we say in Thai; to stay on is lethal, but to jump off is suicidal. So the individual slum dweller sits and moans and wrings his or her hands and takes no responsibility, no position. Or, more accurately, the stand is not to take one. Just give the bad guys money and everything will be all right. That means you can go on doing what you are doing and live in peace, and no one will bother you.

You see, I was taught that to steal, for example, is wrong in itself, no matter whether someone sees you or not, no matter whether you get away with it or not. It was one of those "thou shalt nots." People stole, but everyone knew it was wrong. And people went to jail for it.

There are different rules in the Slaughterhouse. Law in the slums, crime in the Slaughterhouse, and the consequent payback, is based not on legal codes, but "face."

After any incident in the slums, when someone gets caught with his or her hand in the cookie jar, it's not that this is wrong, but getting caught and who snitched, who blew the whistle, and the guilty party may shoot the fink who told, with no remorse or guilt about committing a theft or consequent murder. Guilt, it seems, is a Western way of looking at things.

Westerners have their guilt and Easterners have their shame. Some think we need a benevolent mafia in the Slaughterhouse, a good guy's gang, because the strong here now are the takers and the users. But isn't that wrong as well? Just a variation of "might equals right," except this time, it's my might. History shows that it's just a matter of time before the good guys become the bad guys and we have to go and find another set of good guys.

And the authorities are the same. They don't go out to catch bad guys because they are bad, but simply because if they don't, it makes the authorities look bad and lose face.

So the Slaughterhouse lives day to day and survives on the unwritten laws. Laws that no one uptown really knows about or wants to know about. If you wrote them down, they'd say it wasn't true. It does not—and cannot—happen that way.

Like Lek, the thirteen-year-old rape victim. Tied up and raped in the water buffalo section of the Slaughterhouse. Lek is wild and out of control and her mother's doing long years of hard time because she's already been caught three times. And grandma isn't the lovey-dovey, sweet and cuddly type. Grandma isn't a nice person.

She yells a lot and rants constantly at Lek, telling her she's no damned good, just like her mother. In fact, she says Lek is even worse because her mom was stupid but Lek is in the third grade. Anyway, some neighbors got bombed crazy on booze and *ya ma* and abused this little girl. Never mind what they did. Imagine the worst and you haven't come close.

Even grandma was upset, going to the police four or five times, but things became a bit muddled as the topic of discussion somehow changed from the rape of her granddaughter and why nothing was being done about apprehending the bad guys, to something about the policeman's parentage and masculinity. We never did get the whole story, but grandma is about as welcome at the police station as a hand grenade in bowl of noodles.

This is crime in the Slaughterhouse. Two months later and the bad guys are still loose. We even asked a respected law firm for free advice and a high-class lawyer who knows how to win went to the police to show that grandma had a bit of clout. But money makes a louder sound than even an uptown lawyer can, and grandma is poor.

We're waiting to see if these guys gave Lek the ultimate "jackpot"—HIV. All tests so far show she's okay.

Lots of taxi drivers are still afraid to drive into the Rong Mu. That's just pure reputation. I don't think there has been a taxi driver robbed or abused there in twenty years or so. At least not that anyone talks about. But we in the Slaughterhouse feel a bit of mystique is always good. Keep the curious away.

Violence is a way of life. You just walk with your head down and don't look people in the eye. If someone talks to you, you hurry on by without answering, and if it's a curt remark or a curse, you step up your pace without a peep.

Some of the most vulnerable in the Slaughterhouse are the young widows, usually with two or three small children, trying to make it on their own. I call them "widows" because there's no man around. He's gone. Disappeared. Sometimes because the man has found someone else (younger, prettier, without children) but usually to escape his debt—and the wife he left behind pays or she loses the house. If the children are older, the moneylenders suggest sending any daughters to find some men.

These women have no money to start a business and no skills to speak of anyway. About all they can do is sell food. There are a lot of small food stalls here and the Slaughterhouse never sleeps, so there are always customers.

Profits are not great and if it rains, no one comes. Our Slaughterhouse restaurants are one-table affairs. The real profit is in the booze, especially the local equivalent of Red Eye—bootleg booze, no tax. They don't call it Red Eye. They call it "Twenty-eight" for its twenty-eight per cent alcohol content. But most of the women can't sell alcohol. To sell booze, you need to be established, a community leader, or have enough capital to extend credit to your customers.

Slaughterhouse credit usually goes to the Northeasterners. The single men. They buy booze, Red Eye and Red Bull elixir before they go to work in the early evening, and pay back at two in the morning when they finish killing the pigs. That calls for an investment that most women simply do not have.

The anger over insults sometimes explodes days later, over a bottle of whisky and talk among peers and fellow boozers. That's when the hurt begins, and the booze and talk are like salt in the wound. Usually it takes four or five all-night sessions to bring action.

Here's another rule: a Northeasterner would never take on a local man, someone established here. He would be afraid to do that, no matter how drunk. He would only trash his peers.

These are some of the Slaughterhouse rules and laws. To break them is costly, even fatal. The women, especially the unprotected, matter-of-factly bow their head, avoid eye contact, and suffer in silence, usually in front of their kids. That hurts. To take all that abuse and lose all that dignity in front of your children and neighbors. More shame. Another loss of face.

I can't think of a single violent act in the Slaughterhouse that hasn't happened without booze or *ya ma* as the cause—except for a hired killing now and then, or a case of someone stealing from a heroin drop. That's another rule and it's suicidal to ignore it.

As for the Uniforms, they're not the same as the ones I knew in the West where I grew up. Here the Uniforms are dealers in the game, and the rules are strict. The Uniforms are efficient in the slums. Nothing goes on without their knowledge, so they simply get in on some of the action. The rules are simple: don't disturb the big boys uptown. Keep them happy, and keep the area quiet.

Any notion of a crime-free Slaughterhouse is a joke and not part of the equation. "Keep it all quiet and tidy" is the basic rule. Everyone wins, no one loses, everyone is cool. Except for the Uniforms. They are the wild cards. They control all.

And they keep things quiet. But sometimes, not often, it gets too stifling and there's a crackdown. The crackdowns are also jokes. Because to crack down, you need the locals to identify the locals—but the locals feed and nourish the locals. These Uniforms are funny. They are hungry. They seem to simply stay hungry.

Here in the slums, real crimes simply do not get solved. But we go on—we survive.

Father Joe Maier
The Slaughterhouse, Bangkok, 2004

PART ONE

The Children

A Ride on the Wild Side of Mercy

Up until two months ago, a few mornings each week, just before his kindergarten class, Master Note, a nine-year-old boy in our care, rode his imaginary broomstick horse around our Mercy Centre compound. Note always rode behind his partner, Master Galong, who has a faster make-believe vehicle—an imaginary motorcycle.

Sometimes, Galong has make-believe trouble starting his chopper because Note told him that choppers are hard to start in cold weather. Note is extra smart and school bores him. He is small for his age. You can blame the AIDS for that. Got it at birth from his mom, who got it from his dad, both of whom died when Note was three. He says he remembers his mom who cared for him as long as she could.

Most of Note's life—lived in that deep part of his soul where nobody else can go—seems to be filled with light and beauty. He loves to draw and, except for the occasional fire-breathing dragon (a monster many kids seem to draw in times of death and sorrow), Note's sketchbook is a kaleidoscope of joyful colors and imagery.

Note is small for his nine years, frail and fragile, but he has lots of street savvy. He knows the morning racing circuit with Galong is imaginary. Galong, at age thirty-five with a form of Down's Syndrome, isn't as sure. He likes to believe it's real and who are we to tell him it isn't?

Note rides behind Galong to protect him. When Galong is in his make-believe world, he rides his chopper with reckless abandon. Sometimes the chopper breaks down in the middle of the street, which especially worries Note, who knows Galong has little use for real traffic in his make-believe landscape.

A few months back, Note went through a "bad patch" when his AIDS kicked in and we almost lost him. Spent three weeks in the hospital for communicable diseases. He's okay now but weaker, so he won't be riding behind Galong for a while. Galong was upset and cried until Note told him that his horse wasn't feeling well.

Note, like many of our children, came to us in a circuitous route. After his parents died in Bangkok, his grandmother raised him in Rayong until she too, died, at which point he moved to his auntie's home in Bangkok, where his health deteriorated and he was hospitalized. When he recovered, his auntie brought him to Mercy Centre.

Living in different homes in our care, Note and Galong first met when we took them both to the hospital for a checkup. Galong was frightened and Note, who had plenty of experience with hospitals, calmed him down. A lasting friendship began.

We don't know much about Galong's history. We first found him sleeping on the sidewalk in front of a sleazy back street bar. He would open the door for customers and blow a whistle to wave down a taxi when needed. Apparently, he didn't like his job because without knowing us at all, he asked if he could live with us, and that was it.

He had no earthly possessions, no documentation, and he didn't know his name, his family or where he was from. (The traffickers like them that way, with no identity, so if they disappear, nobody cares.) Somebody here aptly named him Galong, which means "a little bird that has lost its way" in Thai, and he took to it right away.

That was seven years ago and he's graduated from our kindergarten each year since. It gives purpose and order to his life. He loves school and helps the other children. Also, physically he's not very much bigger than his young classmates, so he's not too intimidating.

These days, while Note is still weak, we've asked Galong not to ride his chopper before school, but sometimes he does, and we have to look the other way.

After the bell rings at the end of the school day, Galong likes to help the teacher clean up the classroom. Then it's karaoke time. He changes his school uniform for street clothes, picks up a make-believe microphone, and belts out pop tunes in his raspy voice, but only for about an hour. He's strict about that. Note told him that if he sings more than five or six songs, he'll hurt his voice, and Galong believes him.

Note has been with us almost two years and his auntie visits the first Sunday of each month. He takes his daily—almost complete—cocktail of drugs. The public hospitals enter most of our children with AIDS in their free medical campaign. You have to be poor: we qualify for that. But we must pay for some expensive drugs that are not covered in the hospital budget and ultimately, the doctors select which children are eligible. While the free medicine greatly helps many of our forty children with AIDS, eventually the kids go through a bad patch that sends them spiraling downward.

Recently I've been told the adults can also get the medicine if they are sick enough and have the "Thirty Baht Card," but not until 2004.

But back to Note. A friend to all, especially the vulnerable ones. Recently he's persuaded Galong to join him at art class three days a week. It's a ritual now. Galong (who can't read a clock) waits in kindergarten class for Note to call him.

Galong puts on his necktie for art class: it's that important. He has poor hand-eye coordination, so it was fascinating to see his first self-portrait in pencil (under Note's guidance)—a reasonable likeness, kind of. In any case, Galong was proud of it.

Meanwhile, Note's not feeling well most days. He can't digest his food properly and he has a blood disorder along with AIDS. So it's three days well and four days sick, as they say in Thai. But right now, as I write this, he is well. And every sunrise is a new day—a gift.

The new issue of the day is tattoos. Somewhere, Galong saw a photograph of a guy with a tattoo on a motorcycle, and now he has decided he must have one. Note likes the idea. In fact, it took him two weeks to explain to Galong the story of Winnie the Pooh and how wonderful it would be to have a glue-on tattoo of Pooh. Galong only wanted to know if Pooh would ever ride a chopper. Note wasn't quite sure. He tended to think not.

Note continues drawing. Perhaps his most moving piece is the one of the birthday party with the family he never had. It's among the few drawings Note won't explain to anyone. It seems that the lady sitting at the head of the table is mom. There are

presents for everyone, a bit of cake with candles and probably
brothers and sisters he never had, sitting around the table. It's
a joyful picture. But it's his secret.

When Note dies, as die he will, we will look after Galong as
best as we can, perhaps not as good as Note, but certainly better than the bar where we found him. And we'll do our best
too, to assure Note of our care for Galong.

The boy worries about such things.

Slipping Through the Cracks

Her mother was from one of the old Catholic families in Ayutthaya and was born and raised in the water buffalo section of the Slaughterhouse. The second time she was released from jail, she decided she wanted a child. So she found a man for that temporary union and Tik was born.

Just two weeks after childbirth, she was headed for jail again. She brought Tik to our center and asked if I'd baptize her, and I did. Then she asked if we could look after her too, and we said we would as much as we could.

Many moms care for their babies in jail here but it's not easy, especially for the child. So little Tik was given to us while the courts sorted out her family situation, or at least, tried to. She then went to live with her grandmother until grandmother gave her to someone else. A relative. A friend. She grew up like many slum kids: wherever she could. While her mother did hard time, so did Tik.

We stayed in touch. Watched. Tried to help when we could. Tik attended one of our kindergartens in the slums and completed a few years of government primary school. She learned to read and count, and then started earning her veteran status on the streets. We'd lose track and she'd come back again—for a meal or a place to get out of the storm that became her life.

When she turned twelve—her mother still in prison—Tik went back to living with her grandmother, an incorrigible woman who lied, whined and stole. She told Tik that she had no money and to go out and earn her own. That same year, she was raped by two men. They were later apprehended and at the police station they did what men in that position often do—they offered the police 20,000 baht to settle it. We said no way, we want them to go to jail.

So the men ran away with their wives and that was that, leaving Tik abused, confused and beaten up emotionally. She came to stay with us.

We tried, we really did. We gave her a place to sleep and fed her. Over the next year or so, we paid back all of her debts three or four times. One time, a dealer gave her fifty baht to deliver some pills—*ya ma* in Thai, meaning crazy medicine. Amphetamines. She kept the money and swallowed the pills. It didn't cost us too much to get her out of trouble that time, but we couldn't keep doing it. After that, we said we'd only give her money for food and work.

When she was fourteen, we gave her a job in our street kid outreach program. (Over the years, we have learned that street kids won't let you in, not if you're a grownup—the enemy.) We figured the kids would talk to Tik, and many did. She was one of them. She wasn't paid much and didn't show up often. She'd come and go like always, and eventually stopped coming.

A few months back, she came looking for money. No big surprise. She's fifteen now and says she wants to be a model. She's pretty enough. And thin enough, I suppose, but thin from the streets. But it wasn't for a course in modeling or a nice dress or to hire a photographer that she asked for 1,000 baht: one minute she was doubled over with stomach cramps and dry heaving, the next minute she was jumping around and laughing. She was high on both amphetamines and heroin, and she need money for more drugs. We knew that. She knew that we knew. We refused to give in to her.

So she went away, and two weeks later she was back. This time, she said her grandmother was sick. I said I didn't think so. She kept insisting her grandmother was sick, and I said I'd been trying to help her since she was two weeks old and I got tired of it sometimes.

She said, "I get tired of you sometimes too."

Then she apologized for the way she was dressed. She was wearing a short skirt and a top with a bare midriff, not much more than a bra. She said she was on her way to work at a pub, that next time she would be dressed differently.

Against my best judgment, I gave her 1,000 baht, told her to take her grandmother to the hospital and bring back the change. We haven't seen her since, but she'll be back. We don't know where she lives these days. In the slum somewhere. It's been fifteen years since her mother first brought her to us and she has always come back.

But of course, she won't have changed and nobody believes she will. Least of all, Tik herself. She doesn't have that last quarter ounce of strength or whatever it is that you need to put the past behind. No matter how many times opportunity knocks, nobody appears to be home. The knock isn't heard. Or it's ignored. Someone else's knock is more attractive.

Drugs take care of the pain and what's missing in her life right now. Tik has never known her mother, who finally gets out of jail soon, and her grandmother is a total nothing. All that Tik has had for fifteen years are her wits and her looks, and both will dim in time.

Tik is one of those kids who falls through the cracks, slips through your fingers—one of the almosts, the what-ifs, the near-misses, a poor, sad and heart-breaking could-have-been.

How many of them do we know?

Children's Day

Miss Naree is the oldest of the Gang of Four. She's eight plus a bunch of weeks. Her nickname is Jit. She doesn't read or write very well yet but when it comes to arithmetic, double wow! When you're eight, reading is for cartoon books and something barely required to play computer games. Arithmetic, on the other hand, is street kid survival.

Numbers are always important. City bus numbers, lottery numbers, deck-of-card numbers—that's vital stuff. It's terrible not knowing bus numbers, not knowing where you're going.

Sure, it's easy to get home when you see the bridge, at least for Jit, because her old slum is right under the suspension bridge. But what if the bus isn't going in that direction? For an eight-year-old slum girl, being lost is the ultimate loss of face.

Also, it's dangerous. You might have to ask an adult and that's a risky situation at best. And if the boys ever found out, they'd call you a "buffalo."

Counting fast in card games is also a basic slum skill. Even slum kids who can't read can do double-digit card sums. It's expected of them. When confronted with a column of figures, they panic. Never seen the stuff before. Again, not required.

But they're whizzes where they have to be: a gambling or a business transaction—these kids are cool, never miss. Because bad accounting means you go hungry. School teachers often don't realize that a lot of these kids only learn out of survival, especially kids like Jit, who has no father and whose mother is in jail.

It's not her mom's first time in a jail, but the previous stays were shorter, so Jit could still run the household and look after her two younger brothers, more or less. This time, it's different. Her mom is in for a while and local drug dealers had been using Jit and her brothers to deliver amphetamines. That's why some of the women in the slum had all three children sent to us.

Another kid in the Gang of Four is Ooy. She's healthy but an AIDS orphan. Her dad, who gave it to her mom, died first. Mom died destitute after selling her slum home to take care of her husband. Ooy wants to be a nurse when she grows up.

Miss Ikkey is next, she's seven. Her sister Toi is six.

Together, the Gang of Four hired a tuk-tuk to take them to the zoo.

I really don't know the whole story. The part about going to the zoo is true. Hiring the tuk-tuk to get them there, that's also true. Even the part about them telling the tuk-tuk driver to collect his fare from Chaem, their house mom, is true. It's the part about the baby elephant I'm not as sure about.

The girls said they had to visit a certain male baby elephant because they had heard he lost his mother to poachers. That was their excuse, at least. In any case, they got in a tuk-tuk and said, "Take us to the zoo," which is a considerable distance from the Klong Toey slums.

When the Gang returned, they said they had talked to the baby elephant and told him that all was manageable, that they didn't have a mom, either. And having or not having a mom is irrelevant because nobody is an orphan—that's a really dumb adult word. Makes it sound like we think the kids are helpless, yet they're not. You take love where you can and from whomever you can trust, and if they want to love you, and ask nothing bad in return, that's a fair trade.

As their story goes, they also told the baby elephant that if he could sneak out of the zoo, he could come stay with them for a few days, that they'd work a traffic intersection, clean windshields for spare change, pool their earnings and buy plenty of bananas. Ikkey and Toi told the elephant that they knew older street boys who claimed to know the whereabouts of plenty of sweet grass to eat, but they weren't sure they could trust these boys too much. Ikkey and Toi promised to check out the grass situation as soon they could persuade a tuk-tuk driver to take the Gang of Four back to Klong Toey. These boys they knew also liked elephants so they would surely find the grass.

What they said they told the elephant rings true in parts— at least the part that we just have to look around to find love and protection. That's true for all of us, because these children are just like we were as kids, aren't they? Jit and her two brothers, Ooy, Ikkey and Toi really exist and they tell stories just like the ones we told as children, though in a slightly different form, of course.

But while these kids believe in the power of love and friendship, what they want most on Children's Day is a mom. Dads, too, of course. In their world, to find a mom who combs your hair and sends you off to school with candy money, and a real dad with an uptown job would be the triple-best Children's Day present ever.

Maybe this Children's Day, we can take a lesson from these children and give all of these lost children love and kindness in return. Let's give a street kid a present! Let's go out of our way to be kind to them. It's Children's Day!

Jit has decided to visit her old home for the day. The whole Gang of Four is with her too. Plus her two brothers, of course. There will be neighborhood festivities where Jit and her Gang plan to sell sheets of old newspaper for people to sit on while they watch the bands and performers. Getting bundles of old newspaper for free and selling them as "seats" for three baht a sheet, they figure they can make a bundle.

We are not orphans, they say.

Escape

Her name was Janchira. She was fifteen when she drowned in the Chao Phraya River near the Dao Kannong Temple early one morning. She had jumped off a sand barge that was moored for the night until tomorrow's high tide when it would be towed to the sand pier just past the Slaughterhouse. She jumped feet first into the river. Jumped in for fun after sniffing glue.

Her mom still doesn't know. Mom left on a plane to Italy some thirteen years ago and came back once but without any presents. Janchira's auntie raised her. When we told her Janchira was dead, she broke down and cried and said she hoped the girl could be born again happier, as a good girl, and not have to suffer as a street urchin. Her grandma didn't seem to register the news. The family decided not to tell her bedridden grandpa, who lives in a shack in Lock Two of Klong Toey. He loved her and they don't wish to sadden him. She's just gone for a bit.

Janchira was the best swimmer among her friends; she had also sniffed the most glue. Five of them had been having a Klong Toey birthday party the night before. They didn't have much party money. Just enough for a bit of food, some booze and glue—a Slum Cocktail, they call it.

The next morning, these kids were still bombed on glue and having boozy headaches. Glue makes you fearless. Cut your arms and watch the blood come. You blur reality and think you're totally sober. And so they thought that jumping from a sand barge four meters above the canal into a strong current is beautiful. Yes, beautiful. Because through the glue, everything looks wonderful.

They had no money for a sober-up remedy. Street kids tell you that their best anti-glue remedy are these red, individually wrapped hard candies that can be bought at most mom and pop stores. Other remedies work too, they say, but the red stuff is the medicine of choice. (I won't mention the name but you can ask any glue sniffer.)

To the users, this remedy is important and part of the formula. They say that when they let the candy dissolve in their mouth, it clears their breath. They smell and feel glue-free. That's what they say, at least, and in matters such as these, only the most naive among us would doubt the lore of the streets. Regardless, Janchira and her friends were without the remedy that morning—and feeling fearless.

Janchira often would ask about her mom. What did she look like? Was she pretty? Was she tall? Fat or thin? Somebody in their household had torn up all the photographs ever taken of her when she bolted from Thailand to chase another rainbow. Janchira couldn't remember her mom's face or the sound of her voice. Her auntie always told her that her mom could sing pretty well, not good enough to sing in a nightclub, but she did enjoy singing. In Janchira's fantasy, she had a TV model mom, a beauty. She had no vision of her dad. Nobody talked about him at all.

She wasn't the first street kid to die in the neighborhood canal. There have been four recent drownings that we know of near the Memorial Bridge, all of them kids drunk on glue. Two of them jumped and two rolled in while sleeping. Perhaps there have been others. Nobody tallies this kind of tragedy.

On a Wednesday morning on the twenty-eighth of May, seven-year-old Duang jumped first. Then Janchira and her boyfriend jumped in. Then all three panicked. The two other friends who had not jumped in, Aum and Bam, looked for a rope—anything they could throw down to them. The boyfriend held onto a barge support while Duang and Janchira held onto his leg. By the time a rope appeared, Janchira had lost hold of her boyfriend's leg, and the current pulled her under the barge.

Janchira was wearing her favorite red t-shirt and jeans, which must have weighed her down in her struggle. Also, her left leg was bruised and weak from a recent motorcycle injury. Her friends saw her go under, and they knew.

The family that lives on the sand barge had warned them not to jump. They shouted to them more than once that the current was deadly. The kids never heard them or maybe didn't want to. When Janchira went under, the family would not go into the canal to search for her. Not even the Ruam Katanyu rescue workers would hazard it. It was too dangerous.

Aum, Janchira's best friend, watched everything from the top of the barge. She later begged a few baht for bus fare and rode the number 205 city bus an hour across town, then begged

her way on a baht bus, arriving at our Mercy Centre in shock
and tears. Took her half an hour before she could stop sobbing
and tell her story.

We phoned the district police station to begin the search for
Janchira's body.

By the time we arrived at the sand barge, a crowd had been
gathering since the early morning. We were told we could hire
a tugboat to move the barges and dragnet for her body. It would
cost 40,000 baht (over $1,000) to push these four sand barges,
each ten meters wide and fifteen meters long. That was the
going price. The rescue workers offered to help but said even
they could not guarantee they could find Janchira. We decided
to wait.

She surfaced twenty-four hours later just half a kilometer
down the river, near the suspension bridge. We prayed the first
night in our small chapel in Mercy Centre and the next two
nights at the local temple. Every single adult and child at Mercy
Centre joined us for prayers all three nights. We asked the
motorcycle taxi drivers who stand in front of our building to
watch our home for us in our absence. It is imperative that all
our street kids and orphans know that it is proper and useful
and even necessary to pray for the dead. Janchira was one of us,
a member of our family. Each of us prayed and cried for her.

At the temple, Janchira's auntie and three neighbors placed
coins in the casket so that Janchira would have wealth in the
next life. Janchira never saw her sixteenth birthday. She had
one, maybe two chances to make it and needed just one more.
Not like the ten or more chances the good folks from uptown
get. If you're uptown, there's a bit of protection—family, uncles
who know at least somebody a bit important who can "fix"
things or unravel sticky situations. But on the streets and in the
slums, you have to hang onto the dreams you've still got left.

There's one more thing I should tell you. The night after she died, Aum and Bam, her friends who were with her but afraid to jump in, phoned me at four in the morning to ask if they could come by our Mercy Centre.

When they arrived, they told us they were not frightened but needed to talk about something. Janchira had loved to whistle, and her two friends said they had heard her whistling earlier that night. So we all prayed for Janchira and said that she could come and whistle whenever she wanted, but she should rest in peace. We will not forget her.

We held the cremation ceremony on Saturday evening at the temple. Everyone attended. Everything was proper. We will pray for her again on the thirtieth day and on the 100th day as is customary.

After the ceremony, a local man who sometimes sent Janchira to run his errands stopped by our Mercy Centre and asked for his radio-cassette player back, saying he just let her borrow it. We gave it back. It's worth maybe about 300 baht in a pawnshop.

The Horse Walker

Pim, aged twelve, had been "walking" drugs for six years. In Thai they call these people "horse walkers." She walked them all over Southeastern Bangkok. That's where she's from—born and raised in Klong Toey.

Two months ago, police caught Pim and arrested her Uncle Pai-lawd. That brings the total to sixteen family members currently incarcerated. Only Auntie Nuch is still out but she's wrapped a little too tightly for such serious work.

The police caught Pim as she was walking to the Lad Phrao slum. I'll tell you how they caught her in a minute. First, I want you to get to know more about this amazing little girl.

Pim grew up around rats and roaches—many of them the human adult kind. The kind who live off children: control them and then use them up. Her parents were longtime heroin users in addition to being drug dealers, so they weren't the best of guardians to start with. After they went to prison, Pim had no place to stay so she was passed around the family until she ended up with Uncle Pai-lawd and his girlfriend.

Uncle Pai-lawd started Pim working the Lad Phrao slum as his horse walker at the ripe old age of six. He has two children of his own, but he wouldn't use them. Like most dealers, he followed three basic rules in selecting the proper walker:

1. Use another child in the family, not your own if possible.
2. Control the entire life of the child you are using.
3. If there are no other children available, use your own.

So Uncle Pai-lawd used his sister's kid, Pim, figuring that if she went down, no big deal. The dealers use children like Pim to walk the product because it's difficult for a male police officer to body search a young girl. Besides, if a kid is caught, the child can be sentenced up to only three years. For an adult, it's open-ended and could result in a death sentence.

When Pim first started school, she was exceptional both in class and on the playground; gifted in ways that make other children jealous. She even played marbles, a boy's game, and she won most of the time.

In the beginning of second grade, Uncle Pai-lawd was kind enough to allow Pim to walk the product only before and after school. Later, he used her during the school day too. Before the year was over, Pim dropped out and worked for him fulltime, and when she wasn't working, her uncle forbade her to play with her friends. She knew too much. Had too many secrets. Drug routes and customers' names.

First, it was walk the product before school and then after school. Then it was stay home today to walk some product. She began to miss more and more days of school. The teachers came to visit, but Uncle Pai-lawd wouldn't let them in or talk to them, except to curse them.

That's about the worst thing you can do in the slums, curse them and steal their dignity, talk to them as if they didn't have any, because dignity in Klong Toey is so fragile, even on the best of days. So Uncle Pai-lawd won. The teachers quit coming. It was even easier to drive away Pim's classmates.

There are four slum rules for the walkers of *yaa-baa* or "crazy medicine," as the Thais call amphetamines:

1. Never bargain.

2. Never talk to anyone, especially strangers.

3. Never hold onto the stash when threatened with capture. (Also the corollary—remember where you stashed the product so you can find it later.)

4. If caught, deny everything. The dealer will always bail you out.

On the days Pim didn't want to work, her uncle lied and told the young girl the money she brought them would get her mom and dad out of prison. When you're eight, unloved and have nowhere to go, it's easy to believe such a story.

Pim's first walks were modest in their scope and profits. Later came the big hauls. In dealer jargon, there are two kinds of deals: the regular is just a *dern* or a "walk"; the major orders are called *huu*, meaning "hungry." Pim graduated to making the big, "hungry" walks and gained a reputation among dealers as the best walker in the slums. Became kind of a cult figure in those circles.

Still, in spite of her usefulness, Uncle Pai-lawd and his girl-friend cursed Pim continuously and kept her under virtual house arrest, except to go out on business. They wouldn't even let her sleep under their mosquito net at night; told her to go fetch her own. They paid her only twenty baht for her walks, even though she was carrying up to 800 pills—at a time that they were selling on the street for sixty baht apiece, wholesale for forty-five. When she returned home after a two-hour walk in the blistering heat, they wouldn't even point the house fan in her direction to help her cool down.

Uncle Pai-lawd and his girlfriend were mean even on their nicest days.

Pim told us she began to get even with them when they taught her how to play cards. Even at age ten, Pim was smarter than they were. She learned how they cheated and then simply out-cheated them. After a while, they wouldn't play cards with her anymore.

They had an additional problem with Pim. It's common practice among dealers to let their walkers use the product, to encourage a dependency. But Pim was so young and petite, they worried she might "blur" in a moment of crisis. They needed her clear-headed. That was about the only favor they ever did Pim: allowing her to remain sober.

Sober, yes, but with a weak bladder. It all ended when Uncle Pai-lawd took an order for just under 200 pills. Nothing special. Not a big order. Pim started her walk and on her way, nature called. No toilet was near.

As Pim was taking care of business beside the road, a packet of pills fell out of her knickers.

Police officers passing by on motorbikes happened to see the suspicious looking packets and stopped her. When questioned, Pim observed all the rules she had been taught—especially the part about not talking—but the police didn't believe her. They put both Uncle Pai-lawd and his girlfriend in jail, and Miss Pim came to live with us in Mercy Centre.

No doubt, Pim's old business associates are concerned that she will tell dates, times, places, and such things, but the dangers of her having important knowledge diminish by the day. It's not something Pim wants to talk about anyway. After all, she's only twelve.

Pim can never go home again. In five or six years, when her parents are set free, we aren't sure what happens. But that's tomorrow. Today, Pim's in school and catching up. She's already the third best at jump-rope.

AIDS—Another word for Love

Master Nong is eleven years old and has AIDS. He's one of the lucky ones. He's still alive and loved.

His grannie has raised him so far. She took him away from his mom on a monsoon morning when he was almost one year old and his mom was high on drugs. His mom had been breast-feeding the child even though she had little milk and it was probably spiked with heroin. The slum lady neighbors told us sometimes he would stop crying that way.

Nong's mom and dad were night scavengers, picking up recyclable junk and selling it for their drug habit. They lived out of their pushcart; his mom would sleep in the cart with Nong, his dad on a mat beside the cart.

The day that grannie came along, Nong's mom had left him

face down in the mud beside the red pushcart. A slum dog was licking his face and Nong was screaming. Grannie chased the dog away and took Nong straight home.

Nong's dad died first. Drug drunk one day, he fell onto an object that pierced his lungs and died a month later in the charity ward of a government hospital. After his dad's death, his mom wasn't making it scavenging alone with their red pushcart. She couldn't find enough junk for resale to feed herself or her drug habit. Life had beaten her down. She didn't even fight the police when they found her asleep with a needle in her arm and took her to jail.

She began slipping fast in jail. Grannie begged her to live, if only a while longer so that Nong could know his mother, but she replied, "Please give Nong all the love I can't give him and all of your love, and maybe with that much love, he will grow up to be a monk, even for a day or two. Then my soul can rest." She died alone in prison at the age of twenty-nine.

At the funeral, the temple abbot didn't charge a fee. The neighbors only managed to collect 400 baht among themselves for the four monks who prayed and chanted at her cremation. Three relatives and four monks—that's quite sparse, even in the slums.

Nong's grannie is sixty-seven, still has most of her teeth, and doesn't chew betel nut. She also has a new boyfriend. She's a pretty lady in a Klong Toey beaten-up sort of way. She's been beaten up plenty, but lordy, she loves that boy!

She gets a bit of cash a couple of times a week from her boyfriend. He's self-employed—runs errands. He's never made much money, never gone on big errands but he has managed to stay out of the slammer most of his sixty-odd years. I asked her why she kept him around. She smiled and said, "He gives me all his money."

Grannie cooks a Thai coconut sweet wrapped in banana leaves. It's been her livelihood for years but she doesn't sell much of it. In fact, her sweets are well known throughout several surrounding neighborhoods in Klong Toey for not tasting very good. She never puts in enough sugar. It's too expensive, she says. And Nong eats what she can't sell, which is often more than any young boy can handle. On days when he's down, he can only eat a piece or two.

With Master Nong, life started poorly on the very day he was born with a heroin habit and the virus. He stayed in the hospital until he was weaned from his heroin and withdrawals subsided. Checking his blood regularly, the nurses discovered he was HIV positive.

Nong's mom said that she had no idea, that had she known, she would have killed herself. No mother wants to do this to her child, and that's probably among the reasons she just gave up and died so soon.

Nong knows that he's sick and that he's going to die but he really doesn't know what that means yet. His guts are not in order. He eats and digests food okay but his organs are enlarged. He knows other kids with AIDS. (We have forty of them here.) Our kids don't talk about it, though. To them it's just part of the equation.

You want to know something interesting? Kids with AIDS don't fight each other like other kids, even when they're feeling okay. I don't know what that means. On good days, Nong surfaces at about ten in the morning. We give him his lunch money for school. He makes it to school about twice a week and his teacher gives him some slack.

Wednesday is "AIDS Day" in Thailand. That's the day our kids go to the government hospital for medicine. Master Nong calls all the doctors "Uncle" at Chulalongkorn Hospital, an informality that you and I couldn't get away with, but with Nong, it's no problem.

Master Nong will die of AIDS and we will all mourn him as an only son. But that's tomorrow.

Yesterday, Nong borrowed a baht coin from grannie and phoned me to say he needed an extra twenty baht to call his other friends. Today, some of his playmates at school made fun of him about the virus. He told them all, "You're just jealous."

It doesn't make much sense to an adult, but in Nong's world, it works.

The kids continue shooting marbles.

Children's Court

We've got six Klong Toey boys stashed away in a safe house a four-hour drive from Bangkok. Can't keep them at the Mercy Centre because we run an open house and their homes are walking distance away. We have to keep them away from home, in a place where they've never been before, living by rules that certainly chaff, probably for as long as a year. I'll tell you why in a minute.

In pedophile stories, it's the pedophile the media write about, not the kids: what is it like from their side? That's what this story is about and if you're not ready to deal with a whole bucketful of reality, stop reading here.

The boys, the oldest is fourteen, the youngest barely eight, sold flower garlands and cleaned windscreens with a grimy folded-over cloth at the corner of Asoke and Sukhumvit Roads. That's where they met the two men from Europe. At the time, they were hanging out with Khun Dhaw, an adult Thai friend who also lived in the Klong Toey slum. He gave the boys money to run errands and provide other personal services so when they met the Europeans, they were already damaged goods.

The men bought the boys pizza and hamburgers, and then offered them that first time a crisp 1,000 baht note if they'd come to their apartment. The men didn't ask for all that much more than they'd already given Khun Dhaw, and these guys said they were already falling in love with the boys. Imagine, true love, just like that!

So they did what the men told them to do and got to see themselves naked on the Internet. That's how the two men were caught. Police in their home country saw the pictures on the net and thought the young boys looked Thai. So they got in touch with the Thai Police, who asked if we could help. They showed us cropped pictures. We recognized one of them—a street kid who'd stayed in one of our shelters a year before—and that led to Khun Dhaw's home, where everyone knew these boys hung out. Later we learned that Khun Dhaw sometimes delivered the boys to the foreign men on his motorbike.

Warrants for the men were ordered. One was arrested in Bangkok, the other as he stepped off the plane at home.

The court then asked us to take custody. Now, the boys have no contact with their families because the bad guys have friends who might come around and most of the families are compromised: they took money from the men, too. And they're embarrassed, so if the boys returned home, they'd probably get yelled at. Why are you doing this to the nice men?

And then get slapped around. Banged against a wall.

No school, either. They can't go back to their old schools. If the school knows it's a pedophile case, then how can the kids show their faces there again? What will their friends say? It's supposed to be a secret only the headmaster knows, but you know how it is with secrets.

And that isn't the worst of it. They're getting good care, mind you, but custody is another word for jail, after all. And now that they're going to court, they have to relive the experiences and tell other grownups what the pedophiles did to them.

Because it's a long drive and they had to be in court at 9:30 A.M., our van left the Mercy Centre at midnight, picked the boys up at about four and made the return trip without pause. Court was in a huge building. Try to imagine yourself being eight, nine or ten, and walking into an airplane hanger divided into rooms, then being taken into one of the rooms to be questioned first by a social worker, whom some of the children do know, then questioned all over again by a judge wearing his official robes, followed by the judge writing in corrections by hand in the investigation text for complete accuracy, then back to the social worker. Is this true, is this correct? Then this happened? Do you want to change anything? Questioned by adults some whom the boys know; others are strangers.

The adults were all on their side, but that didn't seem to offer much comfort. It was still a strange place with strange people asking questions you don't want to hear.

After being fed, the interrogation the first day got underway at noon and it went on until midnight—and that was for the first two boys. We tried to make them comfortable, but how do you do that when you have to show them the pictures the men took and ask, "Is that you?"

The answers are often non-verbal. For yes, the chin falls

forward and shows a barely discernible nod. No is a similarly quick movement, head jerking slightly to the left and back to center. The eyes are always dimmed by dishonor, the lips pursed or pressed into a thin line that reveals the loss of face.

Over and over and over again, the social worker and the judge ask their questions, while two video cameras record it all with the microphone on the table open for all to see.

The questions get very specific. Did you have to do things? Did the man use your bottom? Did it hurt? Did he do it more than once? Did he give you a bath? Always there is a painful pause, followed by the fractional movement of head or chin. Were the other boys there, too? Did they see it? There comes another nod. Did you see him use your friend's bottom?

And so the process goes, hour after hour, with occasional breaks for soda pop or a rice meal packed in styrofoam, ordered from downstairs. Meanwhile, the other children wait for their turns outside, bored out of their skulls, finally falling asleep on the floor.

One of the boys said he still loved the pedophiles. Why? Because the men said they loved him. He was the first boy the men had ever loved in the whole world. They gave him candy and bought him clothes, and they didn't holler at him, which is all he got at home. We said nothing. Our job was not to argue or judge, merely to collect the facts.

In one corner of the room, there was a TV set with the sound turned down low. I watched it for a while, discovering that it showed one of the European men being questioned in another room.

He was laughing and having a good old time. He said he knew the law and in Thailand, there was no such thing as rape between two males. Rape had to involve a male and a female. The boys said they took money and went to the apartment willingly, so you can't press kidnap charges, either, he said, even for the one who stayed there an entire month. The man said he confessed the first time at the police station. Why not! He knew that even though he had pleaded guilty and his confession was recorded on video, he pleaded not guilty this second time so the court process would be slowed down by several months, even a year and after that, the longest sentence he'd get in Thailand would be three years. He said he was still in his twenties, what did he care?

At midnight, this wonderful young judge who had been working with the boys since noon, collected the completed investigations of two of the boys and said that was enough—everyone was exhausted. So we called it quits and the boys were given back into our custody and led outside.

Coincidentally, the bad guy was being taken away by the cops at the same time as the boys were waiting for the elevator. The boys looked at him. I have no idea what they thought.

The boys were then returned to the van and our driver and staff took them to the safe house, arriving about 4 A.M. The judge said he wanted to clear this case as quickly as possible so he scheduled another session the following week, when maybe in another twelve hours of questioning, the rest of the boys will finish the same grim experience.

Back in the safe house, the younger boys would sometimes cry. They try not to, because there are forty other boys there too. Sometimes they fight and try to run away. Sure, they're being treated fairly, probably for the first time in their lives, but it takes a while to get used to that as well. They are eating regularly and going to school and they like their teacher. And most of all, they can play soccer, which is the joy of their lives, every day after school. We know that being with other surviving kids, they usually help one another and sometimes, they actually begin to heal.

This, by the way, is as good as it gets for the kids when you're dealing with pedophiles. This is a case where the system is on the kids' side, 110 per cent. The judge is one of the best and the social workers have been trained—and they've gone through this excruciating exercise countless times now.

They've been representing almost 100 children in court and police stations in Bangkok every month. It's a lot of work and painful for the kids, and usually the pedophiles get off—pay a huge bail and disappear—so it's easy to wonder why so much time, effort and pain is expended.

We need to discuss—talk about this a bit. Why even try? There are, after all, other battles to be fought. And after all the court proceedings are completed, there is no damage money for the kids to pick up their lives. No money for tuition to go to special schools. No fine levied against the bad guys to help the kids. No professional help available.

But then, one child with a bit of hope for a new life makes it all worthwhile, doesn't it? Then again, there is an alternative, of course for us too. We can ignore the problem, just walk away. What's left after the courts? The kids can continue staying at the safe house. That's an option. Or if they don't like that, they can come to Mercy Centre or a couple of other foundations for kids, if there's room. Try for an education in a free government school, maybe learn a trade if they can pass the entrance exams.

Yes, a few of the strong do make it. They are the survivors. But to survive, it usually takes a few years of telling them they do matter, they are important. Tell them over and over every day, every week that someone does care.

The others? They slowly slip back to whatever shacks they used to call home and to whatever abusing adults they call mom or stepdad or grandma; or back to Khun Dhaw; or someone just like him, a type that always seems to skate free; or right back onto the street.

The next time you're caught in traffic at Asoke and Sukhumvit, you might see a child selling flower garlands or wanting to clean your windscreen with a grimy folded-over cloth. Let him clean your windscreen, buy a garland, by all means, but before you drive on, remember Children's Court.

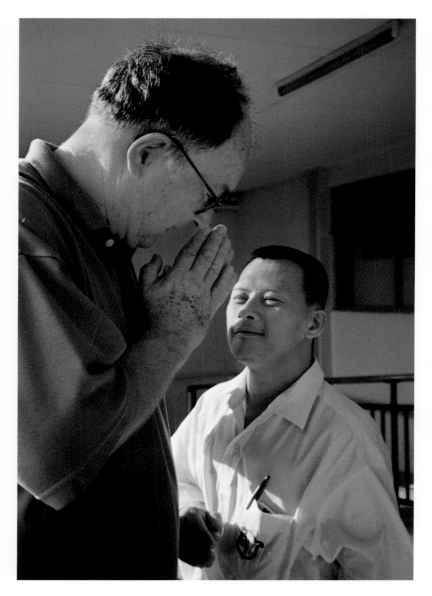

Father Joe prays with Galong, the 35-year-old young man with a form of Down's Syndrome, found sleeping outside the bar where he worked, now a resident of one of the Mercy Centre shelters, and one of the characters in "A Ride on the Wild Side of Mercy," page 31. (Photo by John Padorr)

Clockwise from top left: Another AIDS child learns to paint (Photo by Bob Garlick); Slum children play where they can; Two Klong Toey adults take a break. (Photo by Bill Haggerty)

Clockwise from top left: On a similar walk, Father Joe prays over the coffin of an elderly neighbor who died the previous night and, ten minutes later, is laughing with another neighbor as she washes clothing (Photos by Jonathan Taylor); Some of the young boys play soccer, one of 108 teams organized by Father Joe's Human Development Foundation. (Photo by Mick Elmore)

As many as fifty young children born with AIDS—they got it from mommy, who got it from daddy and both parents are now dead—live in the Mercy Centre, cared for by a fulltime staff, the older ones attending a school on the property when they can. (Photo by John Padorr)

Top: An AIDS mom comforts her infant son. (Photo by John Padorr) Bottom: Girls from the streets, aged three to eighteen, all of them abused one way or another, most physically or sexually, live together in well-lighted dormitories, with plenty of teddy bears and dolls. (Photo by Caritas Austria)

Opposite page, clockwise from top: A typical Klong Toey setting, plants struggling to survive along with the residents who pack themselves into small shacks, and a water jar outside for collecting rain (Photo by Mick Elmore); Narrow passageways wind through the slums, shacks on either side (Photo by Bill Haggerty); A railroad track runs along one side of the slum, for transporting oil and gasoline to the near-by port. (Photo by Mick Elmore)

Top: Father Joe gives Mass to the street kids every Saturday before supper. (Photo by Bill Haggerty)

Top: A bird's eye view of part of the Slaughterhouse, a sea of rusty iron roofs, a tangle of ramshackle wooden shanties slapped up against one of Bangkok's expressways. *Bottom:* Children play in the Klong Toey slum on barren patches of land. (Photos by Bill Haggerty and Mick Elmore)

A flood is worse than ten burglaries and a fire is worse than ten floods, or so goes a folk saying in the slums. There are at least two fires like this one every year in Bangkok's poorest areas, where once the flames begin—often from a candle that was knocked over—residents have less than a minute to escape the inferno, as told in "Poey's Fire" on page 98. (Photo by Virat Sombopsopanant)

Top: The day following a fire, residents begin to rebuild and move a new cement pillar into position for the construction of temporary housing, working through the night to provide shelter ahead of threatened government eviction, as detailed in "The Aftermath" on page 104. *Bottom:* Almost in the shadow of a modern skyscraper, the wreckage of a neighborhood shows that fire respects no one and takes everything, leaving little more behind than a smell that lingers for months. (Photos by Virat Sombopsopanat)

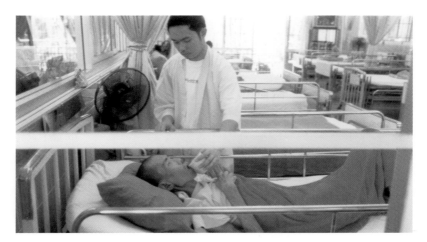

Clockwise from top: An AIDS worker comforts a man in the disease's final stages in the Mercy Centre hospice (Photo by Caritas Austria); Sports, including this tug-of-war, are a key part of the street kids program (Photo by Prapai Sanusarn); Note, the mischievous AIDS child in "A Ride on the Wild Side of Mercy," page 31. (Photo by John Padorr)

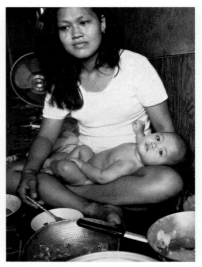

Clockwise from top left: Children abused and abandoned still know how to laugh and dance (Photo by John Padorr); A young slum mom is caught in a pensive moment while sharing a meal with her infant child (Photo by Jason Fisher); A Mercy Centre outreach worker meets with family members of a patient living in the AIDS hospice, offering guidance while communicating AIDS prevention information. (Photographer not known)

Top: **HIV**-infected children live together in a dormitory setting, the older ones helping to take care of the younger ones, along with paid workers and volunteers. (Photo by Caritas Austria)

Top: Young residents of the Slaughterhouse find a flat space on which to play games. (Photo by Jonathan Taylor)

The runaways and throwaways, the abused and the abandoned, find a home and new family at one of Father Joe's street kid shelters; one flashes a V for Victory sign.

First Day of School

The school year in Thailand starts in May, and last Tuesday was the first day. We have over 200 kids in our Mercy Centre homes and every school-age kid attends school so it's a huge day for us, too. The preparations are immense, getting all the kids kitted out in uniforms with proper schoolbooks in hand and lunch money in pocket.

On Wednesday, after the second day of class, already a few of our primary school kids had been suspended. They didn't do anything wrong apart from acting like the seven- and eight-year-olds they are—shooting spitballs and passing notes in class that contained impolite drawings and misspelled words. So we begged and groveled a bit and the headmaster said he'd take the little devils back.

The leader of the gang (I call them the "Incorrigibles") is seven-year-old Lek. He's in second grade and already calculating sixth grade mathematics, but he still can't write his name. He says he doesn't want to write his name and when Lek doesn't want to do something, it's often beyond heaven or earth to change his mind.

Another one of the Incorrigibles is Miss Fluke, also aged seven. Her mom is Thai and her Belgian Dad is a tough guy (and a few other things) living in Chiang Mai. He can handle almost anybody but he can't handle Fluke, and mom seems to be, well, we're not sure where, so she's with us. Fluke said she'd quit wetting her bed if we bought her a new school uniform. She wanted to look pretty on the first day of class and insisted she could never be in the hand-me-down uniform that her house mom gave her, even if it fit. Of course, we found her another one. Not new, but newer.

Lek and Fluke are back in school on a two-month probation with promises of no more spitballs. Nevertheless, Lek was sent home again today. This time, the issue was shoes. He says he won't wear shoes in school. His teacher insisted and he replied, "Why? I come from the slums. We don't wear shoes at home or when we play. How will wearing them help me learn better?"

It was an excellent piece of kid logic when you think about it, but it failed to persuade his teacher, who believes with omnipotent adult logic that a little discipline goes hand-in-hand with learning. So Lek was sent home again, this time only for a day. He's a smart and courageous kid, just not overly fond of the rules.

Meanwhile, Fluke has had to promise that she would stop calling her teacher names in whatever Belgian language her father speaks, but only if the teacher will be nice to her. And so it goes.

We have four children with AIDS entering the first grade this week, and that is so great—one of the best things ever! The headmaster is understanding and says he'll talk to the parents and make them understand that our kids with AIDS are just kids, too, and are no threat to other children.

These children aren't always healthy, though. Even with the most current medicines, they will all die in four or five years, maybe a few years longer if they are lucky.

But right now, today, they're in primary school, which is so unbelievably exciting, especially for the new first-graders. They're big kids today going to a big kid school. It's such a huge event!

Another of our new first-graders is Noi, a bright and healthy girl who graduated in the top of her kindergarten class. She proclaims that she will be a great female scholar in Thailand, and insists that she will be either a doctor or a truck driver when she grows up. In Noi's world, these are the two coolest things you could ever be.

Noi is beautiful but not looking her best at the moment since we just shaved her head of lice. These lice were tough; regular lice shampoo wouldn't kill them, so we had to resort to the old fashioned, sure-fire method of head shaving. No hair, no lice. Noi sneaked back after the haircut and gathered her hair in a box. Later, when her house mom discovered the hair and asked Noi what it was doing there, she said she wanted to keep the lice to see just how big they would grow, maybe even have a pet. She said she always wanted a pet.

So as you can see, our children are not the spoiled kind. Most of them are smart and all are fearless—Lek, Fluke, Noi, and toughest of them all, the children with AIDS.

Every day, our kids show us that there is nothing to fear. They lead us in the dark, show us the way through the grim

Slaughterhouse, and tell us to believe—no, make us believe!— they can be anybody and do anything.

Imagine Noi as a truck driver. You try telling her it isn't possible!

Bad Uncle

Let me tell you a war story. A story of awful combat between a nine-year-old slum girl named Malee and her uncle, a pedophile.

The stakes are the same in any war, only the weapons are different. Malee is the winner so far. She's alive and healing. Her personal war against incest and drugs is over—at least for now. But, Lord, what a warrior! From what we suspect, she fought her war alone for two years.

Malee's savior, her teacher, isn't safe yet and that gives the story an extra twist. Her neighbors in the slums are protecting her at the moment but they can only do just so much.

They live with their own fears and lock their doors against things that go bump in the night, like crying children, domestic abuse and pedophiles. That's why the incest went on for as long as it did—the neighbors wouldn't say anything, or do anything. They said, "It's probably not as bad as all that, so let it go." Malee's relatives said, "The kid is lying."

The events unfolded like this: Malee's mom left her when she was seven months old and her dad disappeared about two years ago, leaving her with his brother and sister-in-law, Malee's uncle and aunt. A few months after that, the aunt skipped out. Malee was left alone with her uncle and that's when everything turned scary. Five weeks ago, it began to get unbearable. Malee had been staying out late at the homes of her friends, sometimes until ten or eleven o'clock, hoping her uncle would already be asleep.

One night, Malee went to her first grade teacher. Yes, at nine years of age, she was still in first grade. She had started attending school when she was four or five but had to drop out and for years, nobody in her life got around to enrolling her again.

Malee's teacher was the only adult she trusted. When Malee first arrived, she looked in great distress and asked the teacher if she could sleep in her house—just on the edge of the mat inside the mosquito net. When the teacher asked why she didn't want to go home, Malee was silent.

That was enough. The teacher understood. She phoned us and we asked, "Can you get the child out right now? Tonight?" She consulted a relative, a community leader who told her, "It's late. Let's settle it tomorrow. I'll bring the girl to face her uncle in the morning."

When the teacher phoned us back, we said, "No way. Get that child out right now!"

In the pre-dawn morning when everyone was asleep, the teacher and Malee ran out of the slums, dogs howling, and hailed a taxi by the main road. The teacher had left her money at home, so Malee paid with money she had stolen from her uncle–money her uncle promised to pay her for the drug deliveries she made for him. Malee told me later that her uncle usually kept all the money for booze, so she often had to steal what she had actually earned, this time using it for a taxi fare to escape. They arrived at about three in the morning.

That same morning, we took Malee to the local police station, accompanied by our house mom. While we filed a report with the police, Malee stayed in the car with other staff. Later, a police captain came outside and talked to her, asked her if she felt safe and happy and wanted to stay with us. She nodded yes. That was all it took (we have a good reputation), and the police entered everything into their daybook.

Just as our kindergartens were closing for the day, the police came to Malee's school to see her teacher. They suggested that our teacher go with them to the station to answer questions about trafficking drugs. It seems that Malee's uncle had influence. Imagine trying to arrest the good guy with a complaint from the bad guy; it's like a bad cowboy movie about frontier justice. It took hours to clear this up.

We also went to the station that evening, from seven at night until three in the morning. The authorities kept insisting that we bring Malee to the station to confront her uncle, and we said that it was against the law. Still, even with the law on our side, it was humbling and frightening. It's the nature of the beast. They are the Goliaths with all the power and we are Davids without slingshots or smooth pebbles.

A male police officer kept trying to assure us that if we produced the child and allowed them to question her, they would protect her. We responded, "You produce a female police officer and we will produce the girl."

They said it was impossible–and they were telling the truth. There were no women police officers at the station, no one

trained to deal in such matters, no rag doll or teddy bear for
Malee to point to where this and that might have happened, so
she wouldn't have to point to her own body. Just men in pol-
ished boots with guns and badges trying to do their job quickly and efficiently.

And they were miffed that we kept saying "no."

We didn't produce Malee that night. We showed them a
copy of the entry into the daybook at our local precinct station,
the one we had made earlier that day, stating that the girl wanted to stay with us. We also showed them a copy of our regis-
tration as a charity. Finally, they let up and we went home.

So Malee remained with us, safe but worried about the
teddy bear she had left at home. We didn't tell her about our
visit that night (why worry her?) or that her uncle had finally
been fingerprinted.

The next morning, Malee's uncle—enraged and cursing his
niece for betraying him—skipped town for a day one step ahead
of the police. Amphetamines and booze fueled his anger and
before leaving, he openly swore revenge against his niece and
her teacher.

Malee's story gets worse. Two days later, the police came
back to the teacher, took her back to the station, and demand-
ed that she produce the child. The uncle was present. When
persuasion didn't work, they showed up at our door with
Malee's uncle! We locked the doors, put Malee upstairs, and
readied ourselves for a showdown. We told the police that any
questioning had to be done by a trained female officer, and to
please go away for now.

But it was too late. Malee, peering down from the third floor
stairwell, saw everything. She ran to hide under her bed, terrified,
and wouldn't come out. Two of our other girls crawled under her
bed too, and they held one another and cried together.

We stonewalled for over four hours until a trained police-woman arrived. Malee was then questioned by the officer in private while some of the male officers insisted on at least seeing the girl. We refused.

It was after ten on a school night and we have dozens of schoolgirls in our home. These kids are putting their lives back together and learning to be kids again, often after experiencing horrific abuse. They don't trust authorities, especially police, and they were frightened of the scene enfolding below them. Even worse, they knew Malee's uncle was there, and if the bad guys can come and take away Malee, they could take away any of them anytime they wanted too, couldn't they?

After thirty minutes of cursing and denials, the uncle shouted at the top of his lungs, "Malee, I love you. I have come to rescue you from this hellhole!"

Malee scrambled out from under the bed, ran to the second floor, and making sure she could be heard but not seen by anyone below, shouted back, "You don't love me. You do bad things to me."

We asked the police to leave but not before berating them. How could they do this? Didn't they have children of their own? Didn't they care about the girl? They seemed to get the message, apologized, and quickly left, taking the uncle with them, while the one female officer stayed behind to explain to our girls that they were all safe. One of the officers came straight back from his patrol car with a stuffed animal he had bought for his own daughter that day. He gave it to us to give to Malee, and she brought it to bed with her and hugged it through the night.

It's not over yet. The uncle is on the run again, and until she is safe, Malee cannot leave the center except to go to school. These days, she's putting on weight, giggles a lot and whispers secrets to her new friends.

This isn't a big, earth-shattering story. It's just a tiny incident, barely a footnote in the history of the human wars waged in the Klong Toey slums. There are good guys and bad guys in this story: Malee, her teacher and our house moms against her uncle and his drinking buddies who watched the incest and probably knew that drug money was paying for the booze they were drinking but in the end, were too afraid to say anything—men whose cowardice overrode common decency and poisoned everything, even a basic love of their own children.

Harsh words, but there is no nice way to tell this story.

The Slum Girl and the Wedding

This is the most fabulous wedding story I've known in thirty-three years as a priest and at least 500 weddings.

It's about a famous model in Bangkok and ten street children she asked to be her bridesmaids and flower girls. Can't use her real name, I promised, so we'll just call her Model Lady, because she is that, a model lady, total class all the way.

She asked these girls—some right out of detention homes, others just off the street, all of them bruised and abandoned—to walk down the aisle with her and her man in church, to be close to her when she took her vows. She bought them all pretty white dresses and white patent leather shoes and took them to a beauty parlor to have their hair done. Some make-up, too, though they were already beautiful.

The first to go down the aisle was Miss Malee, nine years old and still bursting with pain, although you wouldn't have known it on that day. You remember Miss Malee? I wrote about her before—the pedophile uncle story.

On her first night with us, when her teacher brought her to our Mercy Centre, Malee was a very frightened young girl. I promised her I would sleep downstairs by the door that night because she was afraid her uncle would come looking for her. She didn't believe any "adult" promises, so three times she got up that night and shook her teacher awake to come down and make sure I was still there.

She made it through the night, and in the dawn, felt a little safer. (Days are always easier than nights.) The police were informed and Malee's uncle was taken to the station.

Malee would have good days and bad after that, the worst coming several days later. After reviewing the evidence on the uncle's charge, the public prosecutor returned the case to the police, saying the case was weak and the uncle would probably walk free.

The police could hold him for eighty-four days, but after that, what would happen? Even with him in jail, we were paying a small stipend to trusted friends to look after the teacher, who was being threatened with physical harm by the uncle's cronies. He had already made it known that he wanted his niece back when he got out, and he didn't want the teacher to testify. Seems uncle had forced Malee to run drugs. She knew all the drop-off points and he didn't want her to tell anyone. He wanted to stay in control.

The police requested more—and better—evidence. Two more times we took Malee to the police station for wide-awake, daytime nightmare scenes. We had phoned the Model Lady to see if she could come to the first one, but she was working in

Europe at the time, so Malee went with six adults she trusted: our lawyer, two house moms, two legal aid staff and her teacher. But an investigating officer looked like her uncle and she panicked, peeing in her pants and onto the floor. She couldn't say a thing. So we decided to try another day.

Meanwhile, Malee was still in great pain. You could see it in her eyes even when she smiled and played with other children. And knowing that she would have to go back to the police station weighed her down even further.

But back to the Model Lady and Malee.

Somehow, the Model Lady had heard about us and came to Mercy Centre to take a look. She arrived at our front door during a monsoon downpour and I hollered for somebody to let the lady in out of the rain. Malee was closest. She opened the door for the Model Lady. They looked at each other. And something wonderful happened. Malee knew immediately that she had found the most beautiful big mom in the world, and the Model Lady saw in Malee the little girl she once was, deep inside maybe still was.

A couple of visits later, Malee decided she wanted the Model Lady beside her at the police station. She had asked for her phone number earlier and she'd been watching how to use a phone, so she made the call herself. The Model Lady was back from Europe and answered the ring. Malee whispered into the phone, asking her if she'd come with her and be her make-believe mom at the police station.

The Model Lady promised. She told me later that that was when she got the idea of inviting the girls to the wedding.

She said, "This is how I can help make Malee whole again. Feel like a little girl again. My wedding is the most important event of my life and Malee can be part of it. She can be a lady. That's what she needs most right now, to be a lady—a fancy lady."

The Model Lady understood the joy of make-believe and fantasy. And just as she had hoped, the event turned into a true dream wedding. Everything was perfect, even with all the tears messing the ladies' make-up. The groom's parents had flown to Bangkok. They knew about Malee's saga, and they were overwhelmed at the sight of her leading their son and his bride down the aisle. They started crying first, and everyone else followed—tears of sorrow and joy. Miss Malee said it was the nicest day of her life, that she felt pretty and safe.

That should be the end of the story but it's not. Once again, the police said they still didn't have enough evidence. They scheduled Malee to testify one more time and sign another statement the day after the wedding.

Malee agreed to go only if she could wear her bridesmaid's dress and shoes, and the Model Lady had to come with her, too. We thought this was too much to ask her but at the reception, Malee whispered in her ear, and the Model Lady promised again. She told us it was the very best way she could think of to start her married life.

So early the next morning we traveled to the police station, more than twenty of us in a caravan. On the way, we stopped by Malee's school. The school year having just ended, Malee wanted to know her exam results and find out if she had advanced to second grade.

She didn't make it. Mrs. Jiraporn, who has taught kindergarten and first grade to slum kids for thirty-two years, told us that Malee needed to stay in first grade until her reading improved. It was the right decision, but Malee cried, and this time, out loud—the first time she had done that. She had always cried silently, held mute by her bottomless fear. This time, we couldn't make her stop until her house mom said, "Don't cry, girl, you'll stain your pretty dress."

The Model Lady, as promised, met us at the station. She brought her first batch of wedding photos and two gifts for Malee: a Barbie doll and a play kitchen. The Model Lady and Malee sat together on a couch, holding each other, before Malee nestled into her lap and fell asleep. The officer assigned to the case said it was okay, that they could wait, so we all waited a while, a few more minutes, until Malee was ready.

Sitting on the Model Lady's lap and combing the hair of her new Barbie doll, surrounded by the adults she trusted, Malee, for the final time, told the tale of her uncle's abuse, and with that final testimony and her accompanying signature, the legal ordeal was over.

Uncle goes on trial soon and Miss Malee feels safe at last.

What Did Miss Noina See?

Her father was a regular at a karaoke bar in Bangkok, a special friend of the owner, which gave him after-hour privileges with a fifteen-year-old singer named Somsri. An hour or so a couple of times a week of short-time abuse. Sometimes he paid, sometimes not.

That was how this story began, in one of those makeshift bars with bamboo pole supports, open-air on the sides, a canvas roof, stainless steel tables, plastic stools, beer in an ice chest, fried rice.

How did Somsri get there? Her parents needed money— nothing unusual about that. Nor was it surprising when Somsri told the man she was pregnant. Of course, he denied paternity, claiming she was just one of those.

Pregnant fifteen-year-old karaoke singers don't lure many customers so the bar owner, a local thug, came to her defense and threatened the man, who finally broke down and rented her a room with outdoor plumbing—800 baht a month, bottom of the line. He could hardly be expected to take her home to his family where he already had a "real" girlfriend.

Somsri celebrated her sixteenth birthday poor, pregnant and hungry. The father-to-be rarely visited her. Neighbors took her to the hospital when it was time to deliver, and she gave birth to healthy twin boys. The father came by her home a few days later, appearing angry that she was breastfeeding her baby, saying it would ruin her figure, that she wouldn't draw customers when she went back to work.

One year later, now aged seventeen, Somsri is pregnant again. She borrowed 100 baht for a taxi to the hospital, and this time had a daughter, Sumalee, whom she nicknamed Noina.

A nurse told Somsri that she was HIV positive and probably her daughter was, too. In a state of shock, sobbing, feeling utterly worthless and guilty for her daughter's infection, she wailed out her plight, one she later told a sister—how the child's father regularly brought strange women into their home after the twins were born. He must have become infected at that time and then passed it on to her.

When Noina was six months old, her father threw her and her mom out, saying they weren't fun any more. He kept the twins—his sister wanted them—but Somsri could keep their infected daughter. So Somsri hugged and kissed her twin boys and never saw them again. Her young daughter, Noina, never even knew she had older brothers.

We learned many of the events that followed from Miss Noina's aunties. They told me that before Somsri became visibly ill, she returned to work at the karaoke bar. The bar owner didn't ask any questions even though she didn't look 100 per cent. She was getting thin, but she was still pretty and had a voice like an angel, and you'd swear she knew by heart every saucy *luuk thung* song, the sad and wistful upcountry ballads.

Another man entered her life. He gave her a job in his home as a caregiver for his elderly mother. Soon he was having his way with her, too. Yet, even in this miserable situation, she was feeling better than at the bar. She was eating again. And Noina was going to school.

Of course, it didn't last. Like the inscription on the fans that Buddhist monks use during their funeral chants—*nee mai pon*. There is no escape.

Two years later, Somsri looked bad. She was covered in skin blotches from Kaposi's Sarcoma, and like so many AIDS sufferers here in Thailand, had also contracted a kind of TB that settles not just in the lungs but also the brain, giving her a severe TB headache that never went away.

Miss Noina was in the first term of third grade, taking care of her mom in the morning, rushing home in the afternoon to make sure she was okay, and cooking, feeding and caring for her from evening until bedtime. When her mom couldn't sleep, Noina massaged away the pain. (Noina also contracted TB, probably from her mother, during this period.)

The pain and humiliation became unbearable. *Nu mai wai laeo* is how they often express it in Thai: "I can't bear it anymore." One day, she asked Noina to bring home a long piece of plastic twine from school.

It's always best to die in the morning so that there will be food left over at noon and in the evening for your family. The next day, after Noina left for school, Somsri tied one end of the rope into a loose loop around her neck and the other end to the ceiling, sat down, and went to sleep forever.

Miss Noina came home from school and found her. She cut the plastic twine with her plastic-handled five-baht school-scissors, laid her mom down on the floor, and left home crying. Miss Noina had cared for her mom for three years. She was nine now and beginning to feel sick herself.

Her aunties decided to dump her. Nobody wants an AIDS orphan with a suicide mom, and that's how she came to live with us. She stayed with us for another three years. It's unusual for someone born with HIV to live twelve years. Some say it's next to impossible.

Last night, actually at two o'clock this morning, at age twelve plus six days, Miss Noina died here at home. Her heart was enlarged and her lungs were in a bad shape. She had also been vomiting and coughing blood. She was afraid to close her eyes, afraid she'd never wake up. Medicine no longer helped, but we gave her a cold pill as she was developing the sniffles. I guess that helped her to sleep. And so she died.

We dressed her in her new tennis shoes and her favorite clothes and put her in a donated adult-sized casket—the only one available. Someone said she'd have a big room in heaven that way. The casket was of the cheapest kind, made from pressed sawdust. Her aunties borrowed 500 baht to make merit for the monks to pray.

A few days before she died, she asked, "When is my mom going to come and take me home?" Her eyes had that final knowing look—comfortable, secure, memorizing everything within sight, taking in every last detail one last time.

Just before she died, she opened her eyes and breathed her last. I wonder what she saw.

Slum Friendship

Miss Vipa's nickname is Jai, meaning, "heart."

Jai is a high-powered poetry-in-motion waif, skipping, hopping and jumping to her destinations. If there's a tree nearby, she climbs it too.

Just six years old and a star pupil in her kindergarten class, Jai is that rare one-in-a-million child, a pure joy and blessing to everyone she meets. What makes her even more remarkable is how she barely escaped from the tomb. No, I don't mean literally dead, not "hospital dead," but maybe in some ways, even worse than that.

The same goes for her friend, Miss Nang. Together, the two of them truly are resurrection kids. Walking, talking, chattering, jump-roping, marble-shooting kids who are busy being reborn—

living, breathing proof of the birth of a new dawn, and life's magic and miracles.

Of course, Jai, like most children, wants to be a year older. In her worldview, to be seven years old is really ancient. She can't even possibly imagine what it would be like to be eight! She's trying to make the days go faster but she still has eleven months to go before her next birthday. Even with the long wait, she still says "Wow" at the thought of her being eight and all grown up.

Wow! Who knows what could happen? Wild stuff! Actually, though, to tell you a secret, it's not the growing up that she yearns for. It's the cake, candles, parties and ice cream—with double scoops for Miss Nang!

Jai was abused. Her biological father was gone before she was born. Mom and stepdads number two, three and four hammered on amphetamines, beat her with coat hangers and threw her against a wall on many occasions. For a few months, they made a habit of it.

Her mom was sent to jail on drug charges while her stepdad continued to get high. When he couldn't get drugs, he got pure mean (*ma deet*, as they say in Thai) and then he would throw Jai against a few more walls. That's how Jai learned to scream loud and long enough to rile the neighbors and sometimes even get them to make it stop.

This abuse continued until about a-year-and-half ago, when one night, in one of his meaner moods, he tried grabbing Jai's teddy bear from her. In the ensuing tug-of-war struggle, he tore an arm off her Teddy. Jai and Teddy ran away.

She had to protect Teddy and find someone to fix his arm. Teddy was in pain. He needed help. She ran into the darkness, hoping to find her grandma's house, but everything looked different after dark. Fortunately, one of her neighbors had a few

Klong Toey dogs—hardly of pedigree stock but real prizewinners when it comes to protecting scared little girls. She slept beside them that evening until she could see her way to her grandma's house in the morning.

But sometimes, even a grandmother's love alone cannot repair such damaged innocence: the violent beatings took additional tolls and Jai herself became violent. Her grandma, nearing age eighty, could barely cope with Jai's rages. One day she trashed her grandma's shack and broke everything, even the rice cooker.

So the courts gave Jai to us and we gladly took her in. She still can go into rages when the pain and fear return, and then she gets terrible and god-awfully mean. But then a kind of miracle occurred with the arrival of Miss Nang in our home. That's how Jai's resurrection began, but first let me tell you something about Nang.

Nang's spirit has soared since joining our family. When she first arrived, she was legally blind—everything was a blur. Her eardrums had holes in them, so she couldn't hear well either. She was skinny with lice-infested hair and worms in her bottom. She had a bad heart that required an operation, and she was also mentally impaired. Plus, she was born with two thumbs on one hand.

At first she was catatonic and couldn't—or wouldn't—talk. People had always laughed whenever she did. Government welfare paid for the surgery. Her ears eventually healed and she wears glasses now. She also talks all the time and even sings. True, she mauls lots of words, but if you listen hard, she makes sense. She's even put on weight—almost eight kilos—and is strong and healthy.

Jai is like a big sister to Nang, and being a little sister to Jai can't be easy, trust me. It takes time, patience and tremendous six-year-old savvy. Jai has been teaching Nang her whole bag of tricks, all of her street-urchin wisdom, to toughen her up. The lessons started with Jai stealing Nang's lunch money. It's a difficult one to learn, I guess, since it has been going on for several months already.

At first, Jai stole Nang's lunch money even before they arrived at school. Over time, though, Nang learned to do more than just cry and give up.

Now, she fights for it. Nang can't see very well without her glasses—loses at least one pair every month—but when she enters combat with Jai, she is careful to take her glasses off. That's one of their self-made rules. Jai cannot hit her until the glasses are safe. Of course, then Nang can't see and with everything a blur, she usually loses. Still, sometimes she wins.

Jai is tough with Nang but protects her too. Under no uncertain terms will she allow Nang to cross the street without her first putting on her glasses and looking both ways. Then Jai takes her by the hand and they run recklessly through traffic together. Jai tells Nang when it's time to take a nap or take a bath or most especially, when it's time to play.

Last week, they ran away from home—skipped school for the day with three of our other kids and took bus No. 46 all the way to the Mahboonkrong shopping mall. Some kind-hearted person bought our girls fried chicken, and then they did a bit of panhandling and split the proceeds, ending up with eleven baht apiece. Afterwards, they took the same bus back home, quite proud of themselves.

When the children were asked why they ran away, Jai, their ringleader, said that they didn't want to forget how to beg on the streets, and besides, they had to teach Nang to beg too, didn't they? It's basic Klong Toey survival. Every kid knows that.

That was last week. Today, Nang has the sniffles and Jai whomps her every time she uses her sleeve instead of a tissue. In this way, Nang learns the meaning of friendship, loyalty and love. And while Nang is healing and coming out of her shell, Jai learns lessons about love she never received at home.

Jai and Nang are being reborn through friendship. They teach us all.

All we have to do is observe.

PART TWO
Struggles

Bridge to Nowhere

The man who died was named Somchai. Perhaps it was murder; nobody knows for sure. He died from a hard blow to the head. He had been drinking a bit of the Eleven Tigers, a tonic made with rice wine, so some people assumed that he just fell down and hit his head, but the police investigator said that the wound was too deep for it to be a fall, that he had to have been hit with something.

Somchai was a street person who lived under the Memorial Bridge. It's a pleasant spot—a grassy island in an ugly neighborhood. The city won't allow the street people to build shacks on this site, so they sleep on the island wherever they can; sometimes on the bridge itself, sometimes in nooks and crannies in the span's supports. It's not comfortable, but it's a shelter of sorts, except when it rains sideways as it often does. In the most severe weather, they have friends nearby who provide them shelter.

There's a statue of a horse near the bridge. When the street people who live there can afford it, they put garlands of flowers on the statue to bring them luck. It doesn't seem to work very well. Everybody stays poor and drugs are part of everyone's family life. A child fell off the bridge a few weeks ago when he was sleeping and drowned.

Somchai's autopsy took five days to complete. This delay meant that without a body, his children couldn't pray for him at the temple. Local custom and lore say that for the life to come full circle, the body must be present at the time of prayer.

We prayed anyway. Somchai was not the best dad but he was their dad, and the kids needed to feel that there was a proper ending, both for now and in the future, to be able to say, "I prayed for my dad. We had a ceremony. We did what we could."

Those in charge of the case at the police hospital probably didn't think the autopsy was important. What if it takes a few extra days? Who would even consider that a street person has a family who needs to pray for him? How could such things be crucial to anyone?

Somchai was self-employed. He collected used bottles, newspaper, cardboard, empty aluminum cans and other recyclables for resale. Lots of people in Bangkok do that. They're called *saleng* men (*saleng* means "three wheels") and they can take credit for removing thousands of tons of trash from the city's overflowing landfills.

Some claim to make as much as 500 baht a day. I don't want to call anyone a liar, but none I've met has ever come close. Certainly not those who push the three-wheel carts. Upper-class *saleng* men have motorcycles with open wagons attached. Their vehicles hold more stuff and get them around the streets a bit faster and more efficiently. Still, never 500 baht in a day.

Memorial Bridge street folks discovered Somchai's body beside the pushcart he had rented for ten baht a day—a blue three-wheeler, the kind with the wheels that don't always move in the same direction or speed. Neighbors pooled their money for a tuk-tuk to bring him to the hospital. The driver wanted to make sure he was still alive; it's bad luck to carry dead bodies in your tuk-tuk.

Somchai died three baht in debt. He had only seven baht in his pocket and owed ten baht for the cart rental. But the lady who owned the cart said it was okay. She would take the ten-baht loss. Debt forgiven. Sometimes that's about as generous as life gets here.

Somchai was forty-two when he died but he looked much older, probably from the booze. Eleven Tigers mixed with rice wine. Six baht a double shot. Those who mix it use two bottles of rice wine with one packet of bitter Eleven Tigers. They let it settle for three days before imbibing. Serious folks drink half a bottle in the morning and a half a bottle at night. It's supposed to help alleviate aches and pains. Helps you feel strong and gives you an appetite.

Folks on the street and hardcore tuk-tuk drivers know the Eleven Tigers well. These are the same guys who smoke the seventeen-baht-a-pack cigarettes that are way down on the lower end of the smoker market. The roll-your-own, *ya sen*, is cheaper, of course, but indicates very low status in Bangkok slums. Rolling their own cigarettes marks slum dwellers as hicks, upcountry bumpkins.

We first came to know Somchai from the flower market near Chinatown. He dumped his two young daughters there about four years ago, around the same time he figured life had beaten him and most of his chances were used up.

His daughter, Mai, is twelve and her sister, Bik, is eight. Someday I'll tell you another story about them—how Mai and Bik wanted to rent a mom to take them to school on Mothers' Day and then take them shopping in the afternoon so that they wouldn't be so ashamed. Embarrassed for not having a mom like most of the other kids. Most don't have a dad, in any case.

Come Mother's Day and your mom or grandma doesn't come to school for you, it burns a scar so deep, some kids never get over it. Never again will they dare call anyone "mom," even if their father remarries and the woman cares for them.

Somchai kept his son to live with him under the bridge even after he had dumped his two daughters. People think boys survive better on the street but over time, the streets beat them up just the same. He is not mentally impaired but slow and impoverished from birth. Loyal and kind by nature, he went with his father every day on his rounds.

The two girls lived in the marketplace for a year. Women in the market fed them and somehow, the children survived the scary nights. Finally, a Catholic sister from a local convent met them while she was buying flowers for a church feast. They told the sister their story, the sister told us, and Mai and Bik now live with us as family in Mercy Centre. Mai has actually turned into a scholar. She gets nothing less than As and Bs in school.

Bik, however, has a violent streak. Throwing tantrums. Always getting into fights. When she was nine, she was put into a detention home to teach her some discipline. It didn't work. The other day, Bik got into a fight and nearly put another girl's eye out. We took her aside and talked to her: "How much trouble is enough? Your father's dead, you spent six weeks in a prison, you lived more than a year with your sister on the street, your mom's somewhere else and she's married again, you have a brother who's not put together well. Now there's you, and your sister who's trying to take care of you." She collapsed in tears and we held her for half an hour. Maybe she'll go on. Maybe she won't. I'm afraid there's little hope for the girl.

Somchai and his family are upcountry folk of Lao descent—landless rice farmers from the province of Yasothon in the Northeast. He brought his family down to Bangkok in search of a better life doing unskilled day labor and construction work. Moving from job to job, he and his family lived in the tin shacks you see all around construction sites in Bangkok.

Mai, the oldest daughter, pestered her parents to let her go to school because her best friend was going. So they bought her two school uniforms, her first pair of shoes, and enrolled her in a government school that didn't require an entrance exam. She was eight years old and starting first grade.

Her birth certificate and her parents' residency documents were still in the village. Her family never formally moved to Bangkok because that entails a level of sophistication and bureaucratic skills that village folks don't usually have. But a sympathetic school principal decided to let Mai begin classes and worry about the paperwork later.

This all happened before Somchai broke his leg on a construction site.

The day he broke his leg, he was taken to a hospital, x-rayed and had the leg set in a cast. Less than a week later, a fast talking man persuaded him to cut off the plaster cast and rub the broken leg every day with a special healing balm he just happened to be selling. (Snake oil salesmen still thrive throughout Southeast Asia.)

The bone healed crookedly and the construction company would pay only for hospital costs, not for any quackery post-medical care. With a permanent bad limp, Somchai could no longer carry the heavy bags of sand and cement required of him at work.

He lost his livelihood and a place to live. After a few months without a home, his wife ran out of courage and returned to her province, leaving Somchai and his three children to wander the city. Eventually, they stumbled into a small community of like-minded street squatters under the Memorial Bridge.

Somchai started to rent his cart about that time. His daughters slept in the cart at night while Somchai and his son slept on dusty straw mats on the ground beside them. Mai told me that the family had adopted a junkyard dog to watch over them under the bridge. She said that sometimes, when the family had little food to feed themselves, she shared her own bowl of rice with the dog.

Mai suspects that on the night her dad died, the junkyard dog wasn't there. Her father or brother stopped feeding him, or forgot to, or they were hungry themselves. That's how somebody was able to hurt her father. The dog wouldn't have allowed it.

They finally released the body this Friday afternoon. No *sala* was available at the temple, so we asked to use an untended space in front of the crematorium.

When we opened the casket, as is the custom, Somchai's youngest daughter, Bik, who had not previously shown great interest in her father on his visits to Mercy Centre, now cried for him with such passion and thunder that even the monks skipped a beat as they chanted their prayers.

Prayers were followed immediately by the cremation. I then took the *dok mai jan*, a flower configuration made from candles, incense and scented wood, up the steps to the crematorium and said a final prayer for Somchai before placing it in the flames and hurried down the steps, away from Somchai's daughters, where they wouldn't see me cry. I cried for Somchai, the girls, their brother and the mom who ran out of courage, and my tears wouldn't stop. The girls saw me in spite of my efforts and ran over to hug me. I don't know if it was a case of the strong consoling the weak or the weak consoling the strong. Nor do I know which one of us was which.

The next morning, we carried Somchai's ashes to the river not far from the Memorial Bridge, and the girls threw them into the canal. Somchai's son did not attend.

We suggested to him later that he could enter the Buddhist monkhood, as is common for a son after the death of a father. He was shy, reticent, unsure of himself and didn't think he could be a monk; said he didn't know anything about it. We said they would tell him what to do, but he said he wasn't sure.

Last we heard, he was pushing a ten-baht cart, a blue three-wheeler with creaky wheels, searching for bottles and cans.

Poey's Fire

She was given the nickname of Poey, meaning "plump," because that's what she's been since infancy—just a little bit plump. She used to rent a room in the Tap Gaew slum for 1,000 baht a month—less than a dollar a day—until she started the fire. She didn't start it intentionally. She accidentally left a candle burning.

Life has not been kind to Poey. Before the fire, she bought flowers and made garlands for sale at a busy neighborhood intersection. She's thirty-seven years old and addicted to alcohol and whatever else is available to help her in her search for escape. She's not a sex industry worker, but now and then in her most destitute times, she has been forced to find a man for money and food. Her husband had abandoned her years ago, leaving her with her son and daughter.

Her kids don't like what their mom does. It embarrasses them to see her drunk. Since Poey is now in prison for starting the Tap Gaew fire, her daughter, aged twelve, has moved in with her grandmother. She wanted to move in with her auntie, but auntie had a new boyfriend who didn't want complications. Poey's teenage son is now on the streets, surviving by the day.

Her children attended our Tap Gaew kindergarten years ago. They were fun, bright kids. Poey was a pretty mom back then, before the booze got to her. Now she's a mess and looking at a jail sentence of up to three years.

The morning after the fire, neighbors told me that the flames were heading straight for our wooden-sided tin-roof kindergarten in the slum, that it looked for sure like it would catch fire, but in the last minute, the wind changed directions. Our kindergarten was safe. It was wonderful, they said—almost a miracle.

I told them that it would have been far more wonderful and even more nearly miraculous had the school burned down and the houses been saved. It is much easier to replace a slum kindergarten than to rebuild thirty-one slum houses. Besides, in those thirty-one slum homes lived 103 families, most of them renting tiny, single rooms.

Poey used to own her own house, but mortgaged it about four years ago for booze and never paid it back. That's when she lost her children, too. True, they still lived with her, but the love and caring was gone. Her daughter began spending more time at her auntie's home where they had a TV and food was more plentiful.

Besides making garlands of flowers, Poey is a bag lady. That's actually her main occupation—sifting through piles of junk for plastic or aluminum beer cans, anything that she can sell for more booze to get through each night.

Recently, Poey had a new man—a shack-mate—but he's doing time now for drug possession. He was caught with a pocketful of amphetamines, the current drug of choice, and couldn't come up with the "exchange money," as it's called, for the arresting officer.

The fire started on a Wednesday night. Poey had been drinking her supper by candle light in her three-square-meter room. The shack's owner was charging fifty baht per light bulb, 200 baht per clothes iron, and 100 baht per rice cooker every month. Water was an additional fifty baht for each person living in the room.

Poey hadn't been paying her rent for three months before the fire. As a longtime resident of the slum, the landlord was patient and waited, hoping she'd pull herself together. But he did cut her utilities, both water and electric. Slum electricity and water prices are at least double the price of an ordinary meter price—what the rest of Bangkok pays.

Getting water was easy at just a few baht a bucket. But for Poey to see inside her room in the evening, she had to use candles. And without a fan, it was blistering hot under her mosquito net. The TV had been sold years ago. (Actually, there are many renters in the Tap Gaew slum too poor to own a TV, and by Bangkok standards, that's quite poor.) If you don't have a TV, it means that you're not "making it."

Poey had not been making it for a long time by then. I want everyone to know that Poey is very likeable and well known in her slum as a good person. She has always been kind and generous, sharing everything she has and giving it away to neighbors in trouble.

The house where the fire started sat on stilts in the middle of the slum. The interior was divided into tiny rooms, one per family, with the plumbing and a squat toilet outdoors. Folks

wash their clothes outdoors too, and hang them to dry on clotheslines along the wooden catwalks between the homes. Nobody steals anyone's clothes or much else here.

Tap Gaew is an honest slum full of good people. It's the kind of slum you'd want to live in if you had to. Before the fire, comprise 197 houses compressed into a single, narrow ribbon configuration under the expressway. One side faces railway land, while the other side faces a swamp four meters deep, with a few fish, frogs and turtles.

Poey fell asleep drunk on the night of the fire while her candle lit the mosquito net and started the blaze.

The fire lasted less than an hour, maybe forty-five minutes, which is all the time it takes with a light breeze to burn down thirty-one houses in an area just 150 meters long and thirty meters wide.

It takes just two minutes, maybe three at most. When you live in a Bangkok slum in a wooden shack, that's the "grace period" you have to douse a fire. After that, the fire goes out of control. A few buckets of water and fire extinguishers can do little to stop it.

Fifteen minutes had passed before the fire engines arrived, followed by more precious time lost while the municipal authorities turned off the electricity in the neighborhood. (Fire hoses pointing at 220 volt electrical wires are a sure disaster.)

The volunteer firefighters were delayed too, because they first had to rescue residents while trying to extinguish flames. When the electricity was turned off, pandemonium followed. People began running in the darkness for their lives, carrying children and crippled old people to safety and then running back to carry on their backs whatever they could salvage from their burning houses. Everyone in the community was dashing around on these crowded and rickety one-meter-wide catwalks.

It looked like an apocalypse—a hellish vision of chaos and destruction.

As soon as they could, the local volunteer force began to crank up a portable pump that sprayed water from the swamp onto the fire. A few minutes later, the fire engines were set on the expressway above the slum. From that vantage point, they were able to extinguish the flames below quickly. Together, they were able to save over 150 houses in the slum, preventing a far worse disaster.

Slum people live in tremendous fear of fires. They are always on the alert, always watchful, and most fires are put out in time.

Fires start small—from one lit candle or a forgotten pot on a gas burner, sometimes from the cooking grease that's been splattering onto a dry wooden wall for years. Rarely are slum fires started by children playing with matches. Ninety-nine times out of a hundred, it's a very destitute person, usually among the poorest of the poor, who unwittingly ignites the fire, afflicting great pain, sorrow and destruction upon close friends and neighbors.

There's a slum adage: To be robbed ten times is never as bad as one flood; to be flooded out ten times is never as bad as one fire.

It was Poey's first fire. She hadn't yet moved to Tap Gaew when they had a previous fire ten years earlier. Before she was arrested, she was in tears over a lost family photo taken when her children were young. The photo reminded her of happier days, halcyon days, beautiful memories of a slum person's Camelot.

The Tap Gaew community has already rebuilt new homes—temporary ones. The residents are still squatters without legal rights of ownership or lease but fortunately, the land they call home is not commercially valuable at this moment.

The fire has set the Tap Gaew community back, maybe for years, but it's a community with inner strength, filled with families who aspire to make a better slum—like a real Mom and Pop slum, the kind with a couple of paved roads and lots of stores.

How they were able to rebuild will be a story for another day.

The Aftermath

Slum people always rebuild their homes after fires. Always. And as quickly as possible. I'll tell you why in a minute. First, let's revisit the Tap Gaew slum the day after the fire.

You could still smell the fire as you approached. The families that had been burned out were camped temporarily next to an entrance to the expressway that ran overhead. They sat on mats surrounded by whatever possessions they could save. For several of the homeless, the first item they grabbed on their way out was their electric fan. They also had piles of clothing and a few TVs. One boy was playing a guitar.

Some of the main walkways are of concrete and these survived, making it possible to walk between what used to be thirty-one houses, now burnt to their pilings. Not much left was identifiable. A twisted bicycle here and there, scorched gas cylinders, metal pots and pans. There were a couple of refrigerators—symbols of relative wealth. (Most slum people buy their food on a day-to-day basis and even if they didn't, they couldn't afford one.) Several TV sets were strewn about, their guts smashed in. There was a smoldering couch that had been dragged out of one of the shacks onto the barren railway land flanking one side of the slum. There was a dead dog too, its charred remains in a heap. Somebody's pet, gone.

A hose was hooked up to pump water into the walkways where the moms could wash their children. Some people might think that Bangkok slum people are dirty. It's not true. They are as meticulous about their hygiene and personal cleanliness as anyone else, and Thais are known for this. They bathe frequently. So even if the house is gone, the daily bath is not.

In the Tap Gaew slum on the morning after the blaze, many folks who had been burned out were poking in the ashes with long metal rods. There must have been thirty or forty of them, industriously digging for... (Can you guess?) Gold.

In their haste to escape, many folks had left their gold chains and amulets behind—hidden under a floorboard, or someplace else they thought safe. Now, after figuring out exactly where their homes had stood and remembering the precise spot they had stashed their gold, they went searching.

One woman struck pay dirt, literally. She stood up from her bent-over crouch and shouted out in triumph, clutching a mess of melted gold in her hand.

There was to be a meeting in our neighborhood kindergarten because it had the biggest room still standing. The men and women arrived late in the afternoon to talk about what they could do. Some of those at the meeting had been through a fire before but most had not. The railway land beside their homes was an unused bit of urban wasteland. The longer they remained camped under the expressway and delayed rebuilding, the harder it would be to reclaim the original slum site. Everybody wanted to rebuild immediately.

You have to understand something about the slums: they are not always places people want to leave. Given a choice between living in Tap Gaew or in one of the nice "uptown" neighborhoods, there is no question. But it's not a question of choice. Slum people get used to their own community. They form established neighborhoods that have a cohesive integrity. Some slums in Bangkok have been home to families for three consecutive generations, and more or less happily.

This is where we get back to why it's important to rebuild rather than relocate, or be relocated. Everything material was gone, except for the few items saved on the way out of the flames, making it even more important to hold on to the social structure. If people continue to send their children to the same schools, if they continue to take the same bus routes to their jobs, if they continue to shop at the same slum stores, if they continue to see the friends and relatives with whom they have lived and shared a place in their community, then the psychological damages are diminished and their chances of rebuilding their homes and maintaining their livelihoods are far greater.

At the meeting, they were told that the new houses probably would be smaller than their old ones, and that it would take a year, maybe even longer if they had to fight additional red tape, before they could rebuild on their original sites. It would not be easy.

One of the men stood up to ask if they could be arrested if the building was illegal. Another in attendance said that if anyone was arrested, everyone—absolutely everyone in the slum, moms and babies too—was to go to the police station and surrender, confessing identical guilt. In that case, they all decided, that just before they arrive at the station, the moms would give their children plenty to drink and as much sticky candy as they could eat, so that the smallest children will end up peeing on the station floor and leaving messy handprints on the police officers' trousers. Someone then suggested bringing along puppies too, so they could pee on the floor as well. The room exploded in laughter.

We've used the same and similar tactics over the years in rebuilding hundreds and hundreds of homes after fires. During the past three decades, there has been an average of two large slum fires every year, sometimes three, and in almost every case, the people left homeless have rebuilt.

Ironically, in this case at least, the government will be helping to pay for the rebuilding. If the land under the burned-out slum has any value, the government will reclaim it for development, if for nothing more than as a parking lot for government trucks. But there is also a program in existence that provides for people made homeless by fires—30,000 baht for each family that "owned" a house (legally, owning a house is different from owning the land beneath it) plus a small sum to each tenant. The idea behind this is to help the victims rebuild their lives.

The homeless victims in Tap Gaew decided to use part of this money, regardless of the government's original intentions, to build temporary houses on the railway land, starting as soon as possible. It was a Thursday afternoon. The railway authorities who owned and administered the land would not be expected to do anything on Friday. That meant they had until Monday before the authorities could get organized. The plan was to have the new houses up and occupied by Monday when the business day began.

Committees were formed. One would deal with the police and government authorities; another, distribute food and clothing donated from the private sector. A third committee concentrated solely on organizing activities for the children. One more was assigned to visit lumberyards the next day and retrieve cheap nails, wood, and corrugated roofing, much of it donated by a charitable organization. Loans were made and repayments promised as soon as the government could provide its mandated compensation to those left homeless.

The building material was delivered by Friday night and construction commenced right away. Dads, moms and children carried the wooden boards and bags of cement. Tools were loaned to the community. The nine-meter poles that were to be used as corner posts for the new homes were too long to be carried down the twisting walkways from the highway, so the men swam or waded across the swamp with the poles on their backs. All night and through the next two days and nights the slum echoed with the sounds of hammers, saws and drills.

Every slum has its slum carpenters—men who have worked in construction or who built homes in the past. They acted as foremen and told the others what to do. No one slept longer than a few hours.

The last home was ready to be occupied by 6:30 A.M. on Monday, just as the sun was coming up. The stench of the charred wood still hung in the air, along with the sweet smell of success.

Love at the Hua Lamphong Station

Is it a love story or a tale of survival, a heroic cry for help? Maybe just another grim account from Bangkok's uncaring streets? You tell me. But first, let me tell you about Ang and Tuk.

Both Ang and Tuk are drug addicts, not all the time, but more often than not. And they both have AIDS—that's all the time, although even their sickness comes and goes, depending on how many meals they've had recently. On the street, a full meal is two five-baht packages of noodles, easily affordable when the drugs don't get in the way.

They also share a love that burns. Born into desperation and nurtured on the streets, they are eternally bound together in lives whose hopes and dreams have been smashed by a history of childhood abuse and abandonment.

Their odds were never good. Ang's dad died from cancer when he was eight and his older brother died a year later. In the months following his father's death, Ang's mother wasn't coping with life and gave him up to relatives.

By age nine and in third grade, he was already stealing and sniffing glue. When caught by his relatives, he was punished in a manner so scary, he won't even talk about it. All he would say is that at night he had to sleep outside with the family dog.

The relatives turned him over to a local welfare agency that placed him in a youth detention camp. He spent the next year looking for a chance to escape, finally running away by hitching a ride on the back of a vegetable truck returning to Bangkok.

Ang says he always liked trains and that's why he has been living in a shell of a building behind the Hua Lamphong Railway Station, the main terminal in Bangkok. Four times our outreach workers have persuaded him to come join us at our Mercy Centre, but he has never stayed long. He gets restless and returns to the train station, catching the 109 bus from the Klong Toey market.

He told us he has an Auntie—not a real Auntie but close enough, in Chon Buri town. He used to help her sell garlands on the street and always kept her phone number on a piece of paper deep inside his pockets when he went on binges. After the drugs wore off and the loneliness kicked in, he'd want to call her. But he never did. Drugs always ate up the phone money.

Tuk's story is much the same. Her father is dead. We don't know about her mother, not that it would matter much since she gave Tuk away when she was quite young to a family—not as their adopted daughter but as their slave. They wouldn't let Tuk use their family name and when she came of age, the men in the family wanted more, telling her it was her "duty." She was twelve-and-a-half years old and ran away.

Thereafter, what she had refused to give up as her duty, she sold whenever she was hungry and without options. The train station has always been a good place for meeting lonely men. She even has a "train station" boyfriend who helps her find them.

Tuk got into drugs, anything she could get—glue, amphetamines, heroin (they're inescapable on the street) and then got caught. During her time in a detention center, she was so thin and waif-like that the guards felt pity and always made sure she had enough to eat.

Tuk and Ang met at Hua Lamphong. In the Hollywood movies, train stations are often filled with romance and dramatic moments of tenderness, places where lovers part and reunite with hugs, kisses and happily-ever-after endings. So why shouldn't two abandoned, run-away street kids meet and fall in love there, too?

I'm not saying they had anything like conjugal bliss or even sex, though they surely shared a needle or two, which is how Ang contracted AIDS—from Tuk or one of the other kids.

More important than their shared needles was their shared need for care, comfort and love. Eight street kids, including Ang, began calling Tuk their mom even though she was only twenty-one. By that time, she had been living in the abandoned building in the back of Hua Lamphong for almost nine years. Ang desperately wanted a mom and Tuk was nourished by the call. I can't pretend to know what they felt for each other but I know it is moving to be in their presence.

As AIDS bit into her, Tuk sometimes needed respite and would come to us and stay awhile, eat a few steady meals, and get her strength back.

But street people can never settle down, never find any peace of mind or tranquility for long. Every few months, they get a wild urge; there's never enough freedom when they're off the streets. They are like the skittish deer and gazelle or the stealthy nocturnal animals you see on Discovery Channel. Except in this case, as they roam the wilds of Bangkok streets, they search for the next hustle, the next scam that might provide money for drugs or food while looking over their shoulder for cops and other street kid enemies. So it was no surprise when Tuk, like a caged cat, would begin pacing and then leave us and return to her street life as both predator and victim.

Sometimes Tuk and Ang would come to Mercy Centre together and look after each other, and during their stays, everyone in our hospice always felt warmed by their tenderness.

Tuk became a heroine here. When TV crews and student groups visited Mercy Centre, Tuk volunteered to tell her sisters in Thailand about AIDS and her story. She warned them. Oh, how she warned them! She asked the TV cameramen to focus in on her face, and then asked every girl and woman in Thailand who might be watching to look into her eyes, so they could understand and remember.

One time, when Tuk and Ang decided to return to Hua Lamphong, we told them they'd lose face with their friends if they didn't look cool. What we really meant was we wanted to thank them for showing us their love and had bought them presents of new clothes. Tuk chose her first new dress ever. You see, street girls don't wear dresses; they wear jeans. But we wanted her to feel special and pretty. That day, she was even prettier than pretty.

A week later, Tuk was back with us. She'd sold her pretty dress and was feeling sick. Ang had returned too, just days before her. But it was during one of his restless periods when she arrived at Mercy Centre, and he had gone for a walk in the neighborhood. Tuk saw Ang's empty hospice bed, searched around the center, and then took the bus back to Hua Lamphong to find him. There, she ran into her old boyfriend and pimp, who told her he was broke and the police were looking for him—and would she please deliver some pills for him.

The police arrested her and booked her for possession with intent to sell.

As I write this, Tuk is in jail, and we're trying to get her released into our custody. She hasn't told the authorities she has AIDS yet. When she does, they probably will be glad to get rid of her although right now they are telling us her bail is 30,000 baht. That's normal, even cheap for a street girl with a record and two prior convictions.

Without legal aid, she'll be given six years, by which time it will be too late. She will be dead from AIDS.

Ang returned, back from another binge which he spent two days sleeping off. When he first opened his eyes, we fed him and told him he had to stay, that he couldn't let Tuk—his mom—worry about him. She had to know he's safe and off the street and that he loves her.

Chances are quite slim Ang will stay with us for long. Same with Tuk, if we should get her back. And both of them are going to die.

But both are life's winners, too. Tuk knows that we're trying to get her out of prison so that she can take care of Ang, and Ang is equally expectant in his hopes to look after Tuk, his mom. Ang has also asked me for the Mercy Centre phone number in case he runs.

Now you tell me, isn't this a love story?

The Mom Factor

This is a story about children who sell flower garlands on the street corners of the Klong Toey slums, their moms and a new law that is child-friendly. But it's still hard for the law, policemen, courts, lawyers, or social workers to save a kid when the moms and their cohorts won't play by the rules.

The new law is a good one, designed to give all kids a fair shake. It states there must be four parties present whenever a minor is being interrogated in a police station. These four people must include a representative of the public prosecutor's office, a lawyer, a social worker and someone of the child's choosing. (Plus, of course, the police officer assigned to the case.) The questioning must be videotaped and the attendees must all sign a statement before the case can proceed to a court of law.

It all sounds good, but it doesn't always work. Let me explain how the game is often played. Here are the players in one particular case:

* Two moms from Klong Toey.
* Their daughters who sell garlands.
* The Bad Guy who drives a blue jeep and buys garlands from the girls. He lives in a province just outside of Bangkok with his wife and children.
* Two streetwise fourteen-year-old Klong Toey girls. (They appear just twice—once in the jeep and once in a hotel.)
* The local police officers who control the street corner garland sellers.
* The Bad Guy's lawyer, always smartly dressed in a suit and tie.
* Our legal aid team.

It's what they call an open-and-shut case—open because the Bad Guy opens his wallet and pays off authorities, and shut because the case is closed. The Bad Guy walks.

That's how this one turned out. Two moms pandered their own children, pushing and goading them into trouble, demanding that they make street corner money selling garlands, sometimes demanding that they make extra money. This is not acceptable Klong Toey conduct. It breaks the code, it really does.

Imagine, these moms actually encouraged their own daughters to get into the jeep! Two fourteen-year-old girls were already inside. The driver had promised them each an exorbitant amount of money for their garlands, and free candy and toys if they'll just get in. The moms encouraged their daughters to take street corner money. One hundred, 200, even an occasional 500 baht for a twenty-baht garland, the amount depending on the booze level of the Bad Guy.

The Bad Guy abused the four girls: two of them kind of willing, two of them definitely not, and all underage. In the end, their moms and the lawyers ensure that the Bad Guy walks. The kids keep losing, keep doing it again and again as their moms find other pedophiles they can shake down. In these types of situations, the kids almost always stick up for their moms. This time too. Right or wrong, it's their mom—and the kids think they have to protect her.

These moms who break the code think it's all about control. They won't let their daughter be better than them, won't give them a chance, just use them any way possible to feed their own drug habits or to pay back gambling debts. They tell their children, "You owe me." It's like a debt and now it's payback time for the money and effort spent in raising them, an investment. They want a financial return—a profit.

Borrow money at two baht on 100 baht per day. That means if I borrow 1,000 baht from you, I have to pay you twenty baht every day. 140 baht a week, 560 baht a month. You can calculate how much per year. And on top of that, you still have to pay the original 1,000 baht. The moms feel they can control the relationships with their daughters, so they use them. The kids won't rebel anyway.

The two twelve-year-old girls in this story call the Bad Guy the Mall Man, because he promised to a take them to a mall to buy candy and toys (though he never did). Instead, they went to a short-time hotel. The Bad Guy flashed 20,000 baht in the hotel room—5,000 baht apiece that they could split four ways, but that didn't happen. The younger girls got only 300 baht each and the two older girls pocketed the rest.

The twelve-year-olds felt too brutalized to complain. They just wanted to run home to their moms and cry. But once back home, their moms cursed them for bringing back only 300 baht.

They sent their girls back to Klong Toey street corners to sell more garlands. Days passed and the Bad Guy in the blue jeep didn't come by the street corner where they worked, nor did anyone else. Business was slow. The moms needed cash so they decided to make a police report on the Bad Guy, whose license number they had written down earlier. They didn't care if the Bad Guy went to jail or not; they only cared about getting more money from him.

One of the moms came to us and said she needed a secure place for her daughter (meaning, until the payoffs were made). We followed all the legal avenues, signed papers and then placed the young girl in our safe house outside of Klong Toey. She stopped selling flowers, went to school, and best of all, her mom didn't know where she was.

Three weeks later, her mom contacted us. She wanted her daughter almost anywhere except with us. The Bad Guy and his lawyer arranged a kind of contract—offered money in compensation—under the condition that the girl denies everything. We were asked to bring the daughter to the police station, and when she saw her mom, she said she wanted to go home.

Both moms are spending their newfound riches fast. Meanwhile, the girls are still selling garlands on the street corner. They're attending school but doing poorly, I'm told, often falling asleep in class. The case is still pending but it's already over. The Bad Guy, according to our most reliable sources, is now behaving like a model citizen.

There's a lot of sadness and frustration in this unfinished story. I still have hope for the two young garland sellers, though I also fear it will end in misery.

Nobody in control of these girls' lives, especially their own mothers, seems to care.

Slaughterhouse Legends and Codes

Outsiders say the old pig, cattle and water buffalo Slaughterhouse neighborhood at the southeast end of the Klong Toey slums, just where the river wraps around the port, is a dangerous part of town. Some even say it has the worst reputation in Bangkok, one it has earned from decades of crime and violence.

But that is just legend. In its early days, almost fifty years ago, the Slaughterhouse actually was a safe and fairly healthy place to live. Even the pigs were kept reasonably clean. The men did the heavy work—slaughtering and butchering the animals—while the women and children cleaned the guts. The operations required tons of water and its effluent poured into the adjacent canal. At around three o'clock every morning, they scrubbed the slaughterhouse with caustic soda.

There were over 200 families—most of them Catholic, originally Vietnamese from several generations back—living in nearby ramshackle shacks or in tiny one-room homes perched precariously on stilts above the pens. The Buddhists and Muslims have codes against killing pigs, so here in the Slaughterhouse the poorest Catholics were able to find work. Their first church in the Slaughterhouse was just a room under a bridge. Later, about thirty years ago, we moved it to a small wooden house with a corrugated tin roof.

In the early days, you could still fish in the canal. Occasionally you would see snakes, more rarely a few shrimp, and just now and then, a turtle that lost its way.

Nevertheless, there was real life in the canal—whole worlds of thriving ecosystems! And when the yearly monsoon floods came, sure, there was garbage floating to the surface but you could still walk barefoot, ankle- or even knee-deep in water without getting severe infections. Only on very rare occasions would you have to wear Slaughterhouse "slum boots." That's what we call the plastic bags that you tied around your feet with rubber bands.

We had our share of heroin in those days, but everyone knew who delved into such things, and the users kept to themselves. Same with the gangsters. Generally, they loved their children and respected the neighborhood. They committed most of their crime in someone else's neighborhood. We had our local thieves but they received swift and rough justice when caught and then rarely stole again, at least not in the Slaughterhouse. There were occasional shootings and stabbings. (People who butcher pigs for a living know a lot about knives.) But such violence was always against the neighborhood code.

People didn't lock their doors back then. Not that they

could afford padlocks or had anything to steal. It was a neighborhood in the truest sense. Four big families dominated the gene pool, and everyone knew everyone else. The same was true with our Muslim brothers and sisters who lived beside the cattle and water buffalo section of the Slaughterhouse. We stuck together, a bit defiant but proud.

In fact, coming from the Slaughterhouse was like wearing a proud badge. You just have to say you were from the Slaughterhouse and lesser mortals would back away. Even in jails, prisoners who gave their home address as the Slaughterhouse received lots of leeway.

We all understood the codes—the unwritten rules of conduct. The Slaughterhouse codes kept us in neighborly peace while our reputation—the legends—kept us safe from the intrusion of the outside world.

Seven years ago, it all began to unravel. Authorities decided that the old method of butchering pigs, the way we had been doing it for generations, was not hygienic, and that it was time to move the Slaughterhouse.

No work meant no cash for food. No cash for electricity and water. No cash for children's school fees. No cash for mom to buy cloth to sew a dress for her daughter during the annual church feast. No cash for the boards and sheets of corrugated roofing to patch the monsoon season leaks. No cash when grandmother gets sick. Nothing for funerals. No booze money. And not enough for the old brand of cigarettes. Many men and women resorted to rolling their own.

The Slaughterhouse residents were told they would soon have to leave, that they were being evicted from the homes and shacks that their families had homesteaded for over fifty years— that they no rights.

This in a legal sense is kind of true. The Port Authority of

Thailand actually owns the land and most of the slum residents are squatters. Nevertheless, the city social welfare authorities do recognize loss of home by fire, providing the home "owner" as well as his tenants financial compensation. So the laws are rather confusing.

Authorities tore down the pigpens and cemented them over as a massive parking area for the trucks that carry products to and from the adjacent Klong Toey Port. They also wanted to wall in the slum but neighbors banded together and told the officials that they wouldn't accept a wall. If it was built, they guaranteed that no truck, no truck driver, and nothing in the trucks would be safe.

Sometimes a Slaughterhouse threat works and in this case, it won the day. No wall was ever built. But it was a hollow victory.

With the trucks came their drivers seeking drugs, alcohol and temporary female companionship. We no longer heard the squeals of pigs at night. In their place were the sounds of trucks, their engines, their airbrakes and horns (especially their horns) honking all night, and the incessant shouting of the touts who park the trucks and run drugs for the drivers. And it's all happening every night in a dense neighborhood filled with babies and school kids trying to sleep.

The residents of the Slaughterhouse were given a choice: either move into the five-storey walk-up flats the city was building beside the canal (where bubbles of foul-smelling methane now gurgle to the top) or move out of town—way out of town. The authorities would provide housing in new suburban slums outside of the city, miles and hours away from where they could earn a livelihood.

Suddenly in late 1997, with the collapse of the Thai economy, there was no work to be found either in or out of the Slaughterhouse. So the neighborhood women sold noodles and the men didn't do much of anything. Grandmothers and kids ran drugs. Strangers in trucks and their drug suppliers started to appear everywhere. Then more strangers came to buy drugs.

Safety and security broke down. People bought padlocks and had more dogs. Everyone stayed indoors after dark.

Life is grimmer. Every family has lost a teenage son. Some drove their motorcycles full speed into cement pillars. Others were shot by the police, accused of being gangsters. A few died of heroin and other drug overdoses.

The codes are in disarray.

When the Pigs Move

They've closed the slaughterhouse for almost two months now. Why should that be news? Because when they mess with the bowels of the city, it affects us all. The Slaughterhouse slum serves as a barometer: tell me what's happening in the Rong Mu, and I'll give you a "tea leaf" reading of the city, accurate enough to choose a lottery ticket.

No more pigs in the Klong Toey Slaughterhouse.

Some forty years ago, they moved here from the canal near Hua Lamphong Railway Station. They say you shouldn't mix people and pigs. Probably correct. So they moved here to Klong Toey. The Catholics who butcher the pigs followed with their families. Our first chapel was under the bridge. Glorious halcyon days before AIDS and amphetamines or *yaa-baa*, a new name coined by the health minister in 1996 for what had been called *ya ma*. Opium was confined to smoking halls and our elephants didn't die of pesticide poisoning. Now they've moved the pigs again, but it's harder for the Catholics to move nowadays. Times have changed. There's no land. People have settled in. It's a community. This is their home.

So where are they killing the pigs now? Clandestinely. Wherever you can obtain a blurry, but certified ink chop. They moved to Klong Toey when Bangkok streets ended at the Klong Toey Market. Pig, cattle and water buffalo pens made good sense at the edge of town. [Oops, guess I wasn't supposed to say "water buffalo," but since they did and still do, we won't delete it.]

Also, it was down river from the city sprawl—at least the business center part. The offal and water run-off would simply drain into the canal and into the river. We weren't environmentally conscious then. It's better now. We have a BMA governor who tries.

It's a "hygienic" move. That's a given—like, does the alligator swim? But when you go from here, you have to go there. Thus the "there" should include "being hygienic"—a grammatical form meaning an action begun in the past, continuing into the present and not yet completed. Or maybe a "perfect state" which we have not yet achieved.

What this leads to, according to those who dress the pigs, is that the new killing fields are much worse. "Being hygienic" means a blurry ink chop, and the good vets haven't been given a road map. Without a road map, they simply can't find the new killing fields.

Why all this talk of pigs? Distasteful to most. Why? Because it affects us all. You say, good, they don't have to kill pigs. Let them work in the port. That's cool, but the ships haven't been told of our "economic solution by decision" and they don't visit us much anymore. Less work. Hungry kids. Less honest ways to earn food money.

That makes my job as a priest a bit more difficult. It's easy to be virtuous when you've got a secure job. But hungry, a wink or a nod is all the same to a blind pig. No certifying ink chop from the vet in the Klong Toey Slaughterhouse. This was the official slaughterhouse.

The closing was a bit frenetic for a couple of weeks, with policemen confiscating truckloads of pigs on the hoof and freshly slaughtered pork. Pigs in front of the police station, while the drivers negotiated the financial penalty. The hygienic people were adamant: "You can't leave a truckload of pigs overnight at the station." The police said: "We have our standing orders." It was all jolly fun.

So now, Klong Toey Rong Mu folks, with the women who wash the innards, travel nightly to various clandestine slaughterhouses with blurred chops, away from prying eyes.

It seems that the object of the exercise is the ink chop. Thus, those who control the ink chops, blurry or otherwise, control the game. And to mix metaphors: it certainly is not a level-playing field or a perfectly circular pig pen. In this game of musical pigs, one wonders about clarity and lucidity—and safe pork for the citizens of Gotham City, Bangkok. And the mom and pop stores now have to sell more illicit booze to survive. The biggest profit margin comes from illicit booze. Even the amphetamine business is slow because of the tenacity of the authorities here in the Slaughterhouse. The agents are quiet. They say the market is seasonal.

Everyone knows who sells them. Ask any six-year-old. Last week they caught one of the moms with seventy pills. She started with "one leg" (one quarter of a pill) to slim down. It worked—thin in three weeks with no appetite. Her husband, although a good guy, began complaining about their kids always being hungry, and she began selling.

At least she swallowed pills, not smoked or injected.

That rots your brain in a forced march fashion. My neighbor's son was hitting five full pills a day for nine months and he's a basket case. But luckily he's got a good mom. Now—two years later—he's sedated; grins a lot and she can't let him out of her sight. But it's better than being on the evening news holding a knife at someone's throat. We've lost two Catholic kids already this year from the stuff. They were six-pill-a-day men. Heavy duty.

But back to the mom who got caught. She's twenty-seven years old with three kids: third and second grade and kindergarten. She will do maybe seven years and the kids will have no mom. She's terrified. Terribly afraid her agent will find her even in prison. So she reveals no names.

The unwritten rules are: Little fish—the ones who know of these matters—would keep mum, will never say anything, never be witnesses, so that the big fish gets to break out of the nets. When you do catch one, the cleaning is particularly difficult.

The mom stashed the seventy pills in the pockets of her kids' dirty clothes. Her husband now understands why she didn't like to wash clothes and the kids often went to the school in dirty clothes.

The canned coffee merchants and those who manufacture the drink in the brown ten-baht bottles that keeps you awake are having a field day. Among the working poor, it seems that sleep is not allowed—at least if you want to keep a job. Ask your favorite *samlor* or city bus driver which is the bottle or can of preference. Some brands keep you awake longer than others.

Living in the Slaughterhouse beats you up daily. Life is precious, but not very well protected.

Shootout in the Not-So-OK Corral

Nowadays, when people say they're from Klong Toey, they get a funny look, like they've just stepped on something smelly and tracked it on someone's nice, clean rug. The fast food chicken and pizza joints won't deliver here after five o'clock anymore. As for taxi drivers, forget about them. Their policy hasn't changed for over thirty years. No fares into Klong Toey after nightfall. The legend of our neighborhood lives on.

And now our reputation is growing, especially after the Slaughterhouse shootout a few weeks ago.

It all started with a fistfight. Now, a fistfight breaks the Slaughterhouse code of conduct. (We do the occasional kick-boxing but no fistfights!) There are also routine whiskey-fueled fights, but these skirmishes are more of a pushing match, really.

A gent falls down, and one of them asks the other, "And what were we fighting about?" And they continue drinking.

The fistfight broke out on the parking lot for the convoys of trucks coming into the nearby port, on the land where they used to butcher the pigs before the pens were torn down. It wasn't a fair fight. Everyone knew who would win. The big guy pummeled the little guy and when the little guy went down, the big guy stepped on his head and pushed his face into the cement with the bottom of his foot, which is an incredibly egregious affront in Thai etiquette.

It was all about drugs, of course. The big guy told the little guy not to mess with his customers, to go somewhere else and find his own.

The little guy then got up and ran in a whimper down the wooden catwalks between the shacks to his older brother's home only a few minutes away. The older brother was a tough guy, a rogue like his father was called before him—a rogue both in the gangster sense and in the sense of an out-of-control elephant or cop.

Meanwhile, a mutual friend of the combatants who was present at the fight—let's call him the Peacemaker—talked to the big guy, told him to calm down, to be reasonable, that fighting is bad for business. When there's peace, he reasoned, everyone makes money.

While the Peacemaker was trying to persuade the big guy to say he's sorry, the little guy's brother jumped on a motorcycle, rode out to the big guy's house in another part of the slum and proceeded to trash his house. Trashed his new stereo, his new DVD player and his big, new TV.

Here, things got out of control.

The big guy came home, saw the carnage, grabbed his .357 magnum out of a hiding place, loaded it and left.

Folks say it was an hour-long gun battle running down the wooden catwalks in the back of the old Slaughterhouse. Five guns were blazing: one .357 magnum, three eleven millimeter pistols, and one gun "nondescript, locally made, unlicensed" as identified by police from the shell casings. The neighborhood kids helped them collect the spent cartridges. They found thirty in all, plus the "nondescript" gun.

At the end of the battle, one victim lay dead—the Peacemaker, who took a bullet in the neck. There were no witnesses, of course. Nobody saw anything, but everyone knew who was in the shootout.

The police arrested the older brother on reasonable cause. His mom and rogue dad arranged 200,000 baht bail (over $4,500) and he was out in fifteen days.

Forensics proved that the bullet that killed the Peacemaker didn't come from the older brother's gun. He would have gotten out sooner except that the Peacemaker was from a family of rumored local mafia who had asked the police to slow the case down.

Nobody knows the outcome on the case. Most likely, it will be forgotten, like so much else that happens in Thailand nowadays—lost in the sheaves of yesterday's newspapers.

The eviction notice for our neighborhood came in 2000. Two years have passed with no action taken, so the village leader, whose term of office has expired, has not yet been replaced. That means nothing gets done. No trash is picked up. Nobody seems to care.

What's still left of the Slaughterhouse might well be destroyed by drugs even before the bulldozers arrive. Many of the original residents are gone, moving for work in less hygienic and unlicensed abattoirs on the city outskirts. Of those families that have remained—numbering about half of the original

200 families—very few are free of the drug problem. Almost every family has someone selling, addicted to, jailed for or dead from drugs.

Making matters worse, many of the new resident home-owners are loan sharks who thrive on the debts connected to the drug trade. The dealers themselves—most of whom still live in the neighborhood to stay close to their customers—have remodeled their slum shacks and inserted expensive fixtures and furnishings. Plus the ubiquitous rooftop satellite dish.

Somebody recently asked me if the Slaughterhouse was worse now than fifty years ago. All I can say is that the codes here are changing. Local myna birds now imitate the sounds of a ten-wheeler's air brakes.

I hear these birds singing every night about a community in a state of collapse. Last week, a Catholic man died and his family moved his body to a church outside the Slaughterhouse for the wake.

His wife said, "There is nobody left in the Slaughterhouse to come and pray."

PART THREE
Heroes

The Saga of Miss Teacher Froggy

The slum kids in her kindergarten class call her Miss Teacher Froggy—*Kru Kee-it*—and every year she tries to get them to call her by her proper title and given name, three beautiful syllables in Thai. But the name somehow sticks to the roof of the mouth and kids forget it. *Kru* is Thai for teacher and *kee-it* is the word for a tiny frog that makes a loud noise. From early childhood, her mom called her Froggy, and now, the kids do the same.

It's a funny name for a hero, but that's what she is in the Klong Toey slum. She grew up in the Slaughterhouse neighborhood near the water buffalo slaughtering section, alongside the stinky Phra Khannong Canal.

Born cross-eyed, she had reading difficulties in her early school days. Although an only child, her parents couldn't afford to give her an operation. When she turned eight—the minimum age for the surgery required—a generous doctor performed the operation for free. He even paid for her mom's bus fare from the Slaughterhouse and back, plus meals, so mom could be with her daughter Froggy in the hospital for two days during her recuperation.

The operation worked. Today she sees normally with 20-20 vision, no glasses required. Few here remember or ever think of her as being cross-eyed. They think of her only as a hero.

I don't mean that she's the Rambo type. She's pretty and svelte. Her eyes sparkle and dance, and her students think she is Wendy and Tinker Bell plus Kanga and Pooh and Tiger, and even Hermione from the Harry Potter books all rolled into one lovely teacher. She's not a fancy dresser, never owned designer jeans, and mom bought Froggy her first pair of shoes the day she sent her off, crying as we all did, to her first day of kindergarten. She's real neighborhood.

Actually, she was a kind of Rambo once, a year ago this month, during the scare we had in the Slaughterhouse neighborhood over meningococcal meningitis—heavy-duty industrial-sized words for a life-threatening disease that attacks the brain and spinal chord. Three five-year-old kids in the slum got it, and their bodies were covered with bleeding sores. All bandaged up, they looked like war casualties for months.

Since two of the five-year-olds with the disease came from different ends of the Slaughterhouse, we knew the meningitis wasn't isolated to one area.

The health authorities took forty saliva samples and seven more kids tested positive but had no symptoms. Three health officials visited our kindergarten and then walked the length of the slum wearing masks and white hospital coats. Scary-looking stuff.

The disease could have been in stagnant water, garbage or even people's homes, and many of the toilet areas, which were outside and poorly lit.

Miss Teacher Froggy led the brigade. She went from house to house, warning everyone—friends, neighbors, folks she'd known since childhood, as she organized the neighborhood into action. She was everywhere, up to her knees in hazardous filth and pitching garbage into heaps. The Bangkok Metropolitan Authority provided the trucks and we paid for the drivers. Together, the community disposed of six huge, smelly truckloads of garbage in two days. At the same time, we were able to re-panel over 100 toilet areas with new and more hygienic flooring.

Over 400 neighbors joined in the effort. We all took prophylactic medicine and nobody got sick. In the end, the slum was a cleaner place. The folks at the health department said they had never seen a community pull together like that.

The scare finally died down and when the school reopened, Miss Teacher Froggy went back to being a teacher in a slum classroom shack and just an everyday, unsung hero. Maybe this is the most important type—the kind of hero who is always there when neighbors are in trouble or her kids at school are frightened. Some of her students run to her house at night when they need comforting and their moms are still at work. They would stand outside her front door crying and she always lets them in, providing a bed, her old teddy bear, and plenty of love and warmth to get them back to sleep until their moms come home around dawn.

In the classroom, she's strict: kids keep in order or knuckles get rapped. To graduate from Miss Teacher Froggy's second year kindergarten class is to earn a badge of honor. She wants her kids to stay in school. And most of them do.

These slum kids are easy marks, you see. Much more vulnerable than you and I. Many are streetwise and tough kids
but, starving for affection and love, they'll believe just about
anyone who says something nice to them. They're innocent
and open to predators, even when they grow up, even when
they're slum heroes. It's easy to break their hearts. It happened
to Miss Teacher Froggy.

She met a sweet-talking man from uptown.

As soon as she became pregnant, you can guess who was
never heard from again. During her pregnancy, she taught during the week and earned extra cash on weekends by washing
squid for 145 baht a day. This work irritated her skin, so she
switched to washing pig guts on Friday, Saturday and Sunday
nights with the women of the Slaughterhouse as the men
butchered the pork. That paid 200 baht a night.

Now she has a daughter, the glory of her life. She's still
teaching, of course, and many of her students are the children
of her lifelong friends. There's continuity in the slums, you see.
It isn't about transients just passing through.

Miss Teacher Froggy, now twenty-four years old, was a
slum kid who stayed in the neighborhood and is making it a
better place. Still, at the start of every new school year, she tries
to get her new students to call her by her title and given name.
It never works. Even the new kids run up to her, give her a hug,
and shout, "Hello, Miss Teacher Froggy!"

If you were five, wouldn't you?

Slaughterhouse at War

Miss Teacher Froggy called three times in ten minutes. Her messages had been totally clear and blunt as always, but I didn't get it. The fourth time she phoned, it sunk in—and boy, did her words hurt: "Fire!" Miss Teacher Froggy said. "There's a fire next to the school. The drug smokers set the slum on fire!" She was angry, crying and shouting, and screaming into the phone with the noise of the fire and the sirens and loud speakers behind her.

"You didn't listen," she yelled. "I told you three times that the drug smoke was coming into the school, making our kids sick, making them throw up. Now I've got hysterical five-year-olds wanting to run through the fire to save their exercise books!" She slammed the phone down.

Miss Teacher Froggy had taught them that their exercise books were their most precious treasures because they contained their first written letters of the Thai alphabet. Red markings for mistakes, gold stars for getting everything right.

As I approached the Slaughterhouse (five minutes by motorcycle taxi), saw the smoke and met the children, the mob of people and the volunteer firemen, I cried. I'm sixty-three years old and I cried for the kids sick on the drug smoke and now for their ruined exercise books, our school shack and Miss Teacher Froggy. I couldn't help myself.

It didn't make any difference if people saw the tears because here in Klong Toey, everything that is truly beautiful happens, including the ugly. Thus, according to our legends and codes, cry if you must. The slum gives you that honor and respect.

The children led me, pushing our way through the crowd to the smoldering drug houses with our scorched and waterlogged school directly behind. Miss Teacher Froggy was standing with Uncle "Long Ju" Manop. He's the number two leader in the community and all the water dousing the flames goofed up the black dye in his hair so in minutes, he turned gray headed. He's sixty-seven.

Three houses had burned to the ground but were still smoldering, so the volunteer firefighters continued hosing down the school, lest the sparks from the houses burst into flames and burn down the school. Uncle "Long Ju" Manop said in Thai, "*Awt-tone mai dai*" (I can't take no more). "They've hurt our kids!"

Then he told his wife to call his son, who's a soldier, and tell him to bring his friends—Blood and Broken Bones.

The fire was extinguished and the school was saved, but not the exercise books. Water and smoke destroyed every one of them, along with everything else inside and outside the building.

Every child knew how the fire had started. It was an act of arson, spite—revenge, really, against the druggies living next to our school. A middle-level guy, the *yee pua* (the guy who gets things done and knows all the angles) had delivered drugs to them on credit. You know, smoke the amphetamines now and pay later. The drug smokers had not paid. So the order was given: "Burn 'em out!"

Let me tell you how they did it. Uncle "Long Ju" Manop and a couple of neighbors raise baby chickens, training them to be fighting cocks. The roosters are kept apart under big rattan home baskets turned upside down. And when the order came down, the dealers freed Uncle Manop's roosters, doused their rattan baskets in petrol, kicked down the door of the drug smokers' shack and threw in the burning baskets, which lit the mosquito nets and started the fire.

Drugs have always been in the Slaughterhouse neighborhood. It's beside a port where the long-haul truckers park their eighteen-wheelers. So there is no place where drugs are more accessible and more in demand, and subsequently, there is no place in all Thailand that hates drugs more. The citizens of Klong Toey have been fighting drugs for thirty-five years and they were winning until more and more uniforms of all colors switched sides.

Sure, even the tainted uniforms still fight drugs. They have their quotas, after all. Couple of days ago, they arrested Miss Ning. Caught her with two pills and five marked bills. But she's been in a daze for over a week. Pathetic really, didn't know where she was or who she was. Maybe prison will save her life.

But smalltime arrests aside, the drug scene went wild and soon, twenty mid-level dealers started realizing personal profits of 10,000 baht in twenty-four hours. I don't think there's a household in Klong Toey that is free of drugs. Somebody in

the family is on drugs, in jail or dead. Out of 130,000 residents
in the slum area, about 500 are in jail on drug charges. And a
number of them are grandmothers who confessed and took the
rap for their daughters so that the daughters can stay free and
raise their children while grandma does the time. That's common here.

So we fight the war how, when and where we can. I don't
agree with Uncle Manop that Blood and Broken Bones can
wash clean our children's exercise books. But many others do.

Only days before this fire, Uncle Manop and Teacher
Froggy, in the name of the elected community leaders, had plas-
tered posters all over the Slaughterhouse telling people if they
saw anyone selling drugs, to call the Port Authority Police and
also phone our own community volunteer watchmen. If no one
came, they were told to call Radio Thailand to tell listeners
what was happening and to write letters to the national police.
Uncle Manop wrote two himself. His son, the soldier, and his
son's friends didn't show up, by the way. After Uncle Manop
told his wife to call them, Miss Teacher Froggy whispered in her
ear not to do so. Miss Teacher Froggy thought there had to be
another way.

Miss Teacher Froggy showed the whole community how to
fix problems a few years back when there was an outbreak of
meningitis and she organized a cleanup that took truckload
after truckload of infected garbage out of the Slaughterhouse,
stemming the outbreak and perhaps also saving lives.

Uncle Manop is a retired manager of the abattoir that gives
the neighborhood its name.

Asking the two of them to help, we organized a community
meeting for the next evening after the fire. More than 300 parents attended. I wore all my priest robes, which I never do in
the slums. But this time I wanted to make a formal statement—

that this was a war against the drugs hurting our children. We weren't declaring an all out war, not against all drugs; that would be too much. But it was to be a here-and-now war against the scums living in front of our school and directly harming them. My white robes were my battle regalia. I told everyone they could join us or not—it was up to them. However, if they wanted a civil society and safe schools for their kids, they had to go to war with us.

Otherwise, they could take their children home and never come back. We could close the school, move the teachers to another slum school. I was ranting—told them our children were scared and any power we had to protect them had to be used.

My rant continued: this war would re-establish an ethical code for us. I told them the drug dealers and smokers were saying that education wasn't important—that our children's future wasn't important.

So what did they decide to do?

They not only said they were with us; they also drafted an unbelievable document. The first of its kind in Slaughterhouse history. It said the drug smokers were no longer welcome in our slum and we forbid them to rebuild their houses. One hundred and three homeowners out of 114 were present.

Of course, all the children wanted to sign it, and those who couldn't write their names drew pictures! Some of the elderly made barely legible scrawls. Others just laid down their finger-prints smudged in ink. Then Uncle Manop pricked his finger for a blood smear over his signature. That was the toxin and drum beat. We were at war.

We asked for help from the big guys in the Special Department for Crimes against Children and they were with us, too. They ordered the local police to stand guard while the community tore down what remained of the three fire-ravaged houses. The cops came as promised and remained until the houses were gone and cement was poured in their foundation and the entire area surrounding the school.

Residents identified the bad guys both by name and police mug shots—the dealers, the smokers and the guy who ordered the gang to burn them out.

We went to the port authority on whose land the Slaughterhouse sits, asking that if the former residents requested permission to rebuild, to say no.

I guess the word went out. The bad guys ran away.

They're back now, but always slinking around in the shadows. Never near the school. Never daring to approach children. The fire was in April. Today, there stands a refurbished school. And in place of the torn down homes, we now have a large cemented area surrounded by a chain link fence, forming a drug free zone—sort of a "slum patio"—that is bringing more light into the repainted and refitted classrooms, and giving the community an open space for weddings and ceremonies.

Each morning, Uncle Manop waters the potted plants lining the kindergarten playground. The laughter of school kids has returned as they struggle once again to earn gold stars.

There are hundreds of heroes in this story, not just the two names I've mentioned. Even when Uncle Manop and Miss Teacher Froggy first disagreed about what to do, they and all the heroes of our community came together to find their own inner strength in their drug war.

In sharp contrast, during the government's recent national war on drugs, six people were killed on the streets of Klong Toey. Two more are missing. No shooters have been identified. Our first drive-by shootings!

The government's war has changed the rules of the game. Prices are up from about sixty baht to 250 baht a pill in the day-

times and 150 at night. (When night falls and it's easier to traffic drugs, prices go down.) Pills are more difficult to find.
Dealers are more cautious.

Heroin is back in town along with needles and AIDS. The
new cocktail in "time of need" is beer at three big bottles for 100
baht along with a moonshine whiskey chaser; or in extreme
need, the smoke inhaled from burning mosquito coils with
crushed up paracetamol (Tylenol) pills.

And the kindergarten kids watch. They watch Uncle Manop
and Miss Teacher Froggy. They watch the dealers and the
smokers and the uniforms.

Who will make the next move?

The kids watch and wait.

Fragile Strength for the New Year

Miss Kanok-tip is President and Pioneer/Founder of the Klong Toey Slum Chapter of the Physically Handicapped, that is, the Five Kiosk Workforce.

At thirty-eight years of age, she's tough in some ways but very fragile in others. Never went to school. Lost one leg from bone cancer years ago. Just recently her husband, while working as an assistant bartender, began a relationship with a short-time girl from a remote province who hires herself out of the bar and he just left Kanok-tip. One other thing: Tip is four months pregnant.

Pregnant Tip may be going through a bad patch, but she's a Klong Toey woman. Chances are she'll come out of it with only a few new emotional scars. She lives with her mom and ten-year-old daughter in the house her mom and dad homesteaded in Lock One in the Klong Toey slum almost thirty years ago.

Now, Miss Kanok-tip and her handicapped Chapter control and manage the five kiosks on the main road running through the slum. They hold monthly meetings and make themselves known in the community. They have pride in what they do. Earning respectable livelihoods, they see themselves as first class (no longer second class) citizens. True, the sales of soft drinks and power drinks have plummeted since the 2003 drug wars started and killed off their night trade. But they keep trying.

These are fragile moments in Klong Toey society, where the most common New Year's blessing seems to be, "May you be money rich." Where interest rates are two per cent per day and perhaps on New Year's day, a moneylender in a weak moment of largess might say you don't have to pay interest today on your loan—but probably not. Where the respect you receive and the *wai* you are greeted with are based on money and power, not age or merit.

Folks don't *wai* Miss Kanok-tip very often. It's not terribly fashionable to *wai* the crippled poor. Plus the fact that Miss Kanok-tip is from one of those large old Klong Toey families that neighbors know only by first names. And even if they did know her last name, it wouldn't be an impressive one, at least not in a money-rich way.

To say that the opinion of others—what they say or don't say about you—is not important, that's garbage. It hurts when people ignore you. And that's what makes Miss Kanok-tip and her Chapter so very fragile and so very important. Fragile, because it's next to impossible to survive economically on their five donated kiosks. And important, because their Chapter brings pride and self respect to the handicapped of Klong Toey and all other slums. They refuse to be ignored.

And they refuse to give up. They struggle every day, often just to get out of bed in the morning, dress, and onto their wheelchairs. Not living in handicapped-friendly homes, but in Klong Toey shacks, they negotiate inhospitable streets, lanes and broken sidewalks, hand-pushing their wheelchairs every morning to get to work, put in twelve hours, and make just enough profit to restock supplies for the next day—day after day.

Economics aside, Miss Tip and her pioneer Chapter have made a quantum leap forward and are moving at warp speed. It takes great courage to make their own way in the slums and say, "Hey, look at us, Klong Toey. We belong here! We can't read or write, and we can't walk, but we are Klong Toey."

You might wonder how they can operate five kiosks if they are illiterate? But they can sign their names and they can count in every direction. (Miss Kanok-tip learned how to count watching neighborhood women playing cards!)

As always, though, it's a fragile situation. With a wobbly government-issued wheelchair, bent crutches, no additional household income, no husband, no money in the bank and no schooling, Miss Kanok-tip is trying to make it on her own in her own way. To do that honestly—without selling drugs or the Three K glue in the green cans or the throw-away cigarette lighters that you sniff the gas from—that's extremely fragile. Meanwhile, she is raising a daughter who is near the top of her class in school and aspires to be a classical Thai dancer; and she's determined to give her second child a better future.

Fortunately, Miss Kanok-tip knows how to sell. As a child, she always stayed at home with her mom, who sold cigarettes—one or two at a time, occasionally a full pack. Sold locally made booze too, by the shot glass. Nothing really taxable.

Mom never sold food because her eleven children, including Tip who was number five, would eat all the food before she could sell it. Mom never went to school, but she could count. Seems all slum moms know how to count.

Tip remembers her dad fondly. He would gently pick her up every morning and place her in her wheelchair before he went off to the port to look for day labor, which usually involved carrying eighty-kilogram rice sacks up and down gangplanks. He told her many times, "Tip my beloved, special daughter, never give up hope. Never stop trying."

It couldn't have been easy to believe her dad. Imagine if ever since you can remember, it was drilled into you daily that your ailments made you second class and that it was your own fault, probably because of some sins you committed in a previous lifetime. Brainwashed in this way, you become—and remain—always fragile.

It's surely worse for Tip since her husband walked. Back when she was twenty-six, no one had ever told her she was pretty, so she was beguiled by a sweet-talking guy. She got pregnant. Her dad had a conversation with the guy, and he stayed. Later, her husband learned how to be an assistant bartender and left her for another.

But life goes on.

Current matters in the slums aren't helping business at all. Since the 2003 drug wars started, kiosk sales are way down. No one is around after dark to buy anything. People are afraid of strangers riding by on motorcycles. Mostly, they're afraid of the strangers' guns. When the kiosks are able to stay open twelve hours a day, they average only 150 baht total sales, and their profit has to come from that. It's a fragile livelihood. Economically, it's the pits.

Yet somehow, fragile or not, Tip and her Five Kiosk Workforce are the strength of the new Klong Toey. They are both pioneers and heroes. How does that storyline from the TV show go? Something like...they dare to go where no one else has gone before. We—you and I—the children born of lesser gods, cannot afford to lose them.

Klong Toey is a sacred place (it means "Canal of the Pandanus Leaves" in Thai). A place where people like Miss Kanok-tip on her wobbly wheelchair and her bent crutches can not only survive but even prosper, albeit in a humble Klong Toey way. If you are passing by, stop by and buy a soft drink. And if you wish, please do wish her and her Chapter a happy and prosperous New Year.

Their strength is our future.

Samlee's Triumph

"All of your stories are so sad," a friend said. "Are there any happy stories in the Bangkok slums?"

He's from a nice neighborhood, doesn't know Klong Toey, so I gave him the benefit of the doubt and told him the happiest story I could think of at the moment—about a thirty-one-year-old woman named Samlee.

She and her older sister grew up in the care of her Uncle Shorty and Auntie Tanom. She barely remembers her mom. Only that her name was Vipa and that she was petite and beautiful with a lovely complexion and long, black hair flowing down her shoulders. She remembers her dad better. He would come by the first day of every month and leave money with Uncle Shorty and Auntie Tanom to take care of his children. She remembers him as tall and scary looking but gentle when he held her.

Samlee was always told to call him "uncle," and she only found out the truth years later. She didn't understand why he would only visit at night and always avoided windows and bright lights. He came alone, never with Samlee's mom, who would visit during the day. Samlee's father was a notorious gangster, a hit man, feared by all and always hunted by police.

While Samlee was still a child, one day, the first of the month came and passed and he didn't show up. He never returned. The next time her mother visited, she was dressed in black, her face red with tears. Samlee never saw her mother again, either.

Uncle Shorty homesteaded under the Three Solders Bridge by the railroad tracks near the Slaughterhouse. Their home was always damp with the canal water, most of it coming from the passing long tail boats whose wakes splashed into the side of their shack. Like all the children living under the bridge, she swam and bathed in the canal, which led to skin infections that took years—until young adulthood—to heal.

The family had one light bulb, one fan, one rice-cooker, one mosquito net, one plastic clothes container, and one wooden food cabinet with bowls filled with water beneath its legs to keep the ants from climbing up into the food. No refrigerator. No gas stove. No TV. Not even a radio.

Their only source of drinking and washing water was at the slaughterhouse, where Samlee went twice a day from early childhood on, hauling buckets back home. The slaughterhouse water supply would be turned on when work began at eight o'clock in the evening. On Sundays, when religious custom forbids the slaughtering of animals, they didn't turn on the water until after midnight.

Fifty-four families lived under that bridge. Samlee was the prettiest girl and Uncle Shorty was the most respected man. He rolled his own cigarettes and the smoke eventually killed him. He only drank beer on rare occasions after he got paid for a carpentry job, and almost all of his money went toward his family. Family always came first.

Uncle Shorty tried to instill in Samlee and her sister a sense of pride. He gave them his family name and told the children that they were Klong Toey girls and to be proud of it—to be proud of their home and family.

Samlee was a month into first grade when Auntie Tanom died. Uncle Shorty kept her body at home for two days, as he didn't have any money to pray at the temple. The neighbors brought in a cot to place the body on because the high river tides sometimes flooded the shack. Uncle Shorty in his love and grief was worried that mosquitoes might bother Auntie Tanom, so the whole family slept next to her body under the mosquito net.

The family went to a Chinese benevolent society for a donated casket, the cheapest kind made, and carried Auntie Tanom to the temple for cremation. After Auntie Tanom died, Samlee's older sister, though only in sixth grade, quit school and went to live with a man. Said she was tired of being poor.

Samlee finished her six years of grammar school near the top of her class. That same year, the city evicted the fifty-four families living under the bridge, and Samlee and Uncle Shorty were relocated to another home in Klong Toey.

When Samlee graduated from high school, she entered a polytechnic college but had to drop out during the second year. Uncle Shorty was sick. Her favorite professor told her to come back when she could but for the next two years, Samlee took care of her Uncle Shorty, bringing him back and forth to a government hospital four different times. Samlee was almost eighteen when Uncle Shorty died.

Before long, she met a sweet-talking man from the Flats in Klong Toey. He took her to the beach for a weekend and then moved into her house, the one Uncle Shorty left her. There was no wedding ceremony. No dowry. No respect. And he wasn't faithful. During her first pregnancy, she knew she wanted to throw him out but decided to devote all her strength and energy to her child.

When it was time to go to the hospital, he was hanging out somewhere else, so neighborhood women took her there. After her son was born, she gave the boyfriend the boot.

Samlee needed money, so she found a friend who could care for her baby while she took on temporary work. At her new job, she met another man, this one handsome and a high school graduate with a fulltime job.

Their first three years together were happy and a second child was born, this time a daughter. After that, Samlee applied for a teaching job at one of our kindergartens and we accepted her immediately.

Unfortunately, her husband began playing with drugs, copping from an uncle who was a dealer. Then he lost his job. Then he began selling the stuff. And then, when Samlee went to teach in the mornings, he began taking their baby on his rounds. Samlee knew nothing of this until her husband was caught. Seven different times she went to court on this case, pleading on his behalf, paying fees and fines, and eventually, mortgaging the home.

So when, exactly, does this story get happy, you're probably asking.

After the trial, the husband continued on his downward spiral, this time with amphetamines. Took up to twelve pills a day, which is almost unbelievable. Of course, he got caught again and this time, went to prison for a long stretch.

Samlee seized the opportunity. She got a divorce and applied for a loan from our slum women's credit union to get her life out of hock. She promised she would continue teaching kindergarten and pay back the loan from her wages. Today, she's keeping her promise.

Protective of her children and fearing the influence of the neighborhood drug problem, Samlee has moved her family out near the airport in an area the city has designated for slum relocation. Both of her children excel in school. Her ten-year-old daughter is always near the top of her class—one year, even first! Her son is in high school and likes boxing, computers and English, in that order.

Samlee's story is happy in a Klong Toey way. She's our kind of hero. Beaten up but never beaten, Samlee never (not once!) ever thought of quitting. If we hadn't helped her, she would have found another way on her own. Uncle Shorty was a fine role model and Samlee was paying attention. (Her older sister, sad to say, didn't have the same drive. She recently died of AIDS in our hospice.)

There's a popular rock ballad in America about a rose in Spanish Harlem. That's our Samlee—an orchid in the Thai slums. Most folks see the filth, drugs and hopelessness in Klong Toey, but in a kindergarten classroom here five mornings every week, there stands a thirty-one-year-old teacher who loves her children and tries with all her heart to give each of them a sense of pride in the Klong Toey slum, just as her Uncle Shorty did before her. She's even changed her family name back to Uncle Shorty's and changed her kids' names, too.

And that's what I call a happy story.

About The Human Development Foundation

How We Help

The Human Development Foundation, a non-denominational, community-based organization, began in 1974 with the works of Father Joe Maier and Sister Maria Chantavarodom in Klong Toey, Bangkok's largest slum. Their first project was a one-baht-per-day kindergarten. Within the next two years, they opened Klong Toey's first outreach health clinic as well as a shelter for street children.

Fires devastated slum neighborhoods sometimes two or three times a year, and the HDF helped rebuild them.

Over the past thirty years, the foundation has continuously initiated projects to help the poor. When a pilot program worked in one neighborhood, it was expanded to another, and in this way, with a staff of 280 dedicated men and women, the HDF now reaches out to friends in over thirty slum communities in Bangkok.

Mercy Centre

Mercy Centre is a shelter for street kids, a home for mothers and children with HIV/AIDS, a respite hospice for adults with AIDS, a community meeting place, and a serene haven in the slums with small gardens and playgrounds. Originally built on a forsaken piece of port authority property, Mercy Centre has stood as a sign that somebody actually cares—first a shack church school and a rented slum house for street kids, then a crowded AIDS hospice—always changing and always the same for thirty years. In 2000, it was rebuilt through a generous gift to accommodate our expanding services to orphans, street children and children with HIV/AIDS.

Father Joe Maier, Founder and Director

Father Joseph Maier, C.Ss.R., has lived among the poor in

Thailand and Laos since 1967. He settled in Bangkok in the early seventies where he served as the priest to a small Catholic parish in the Slaughterhouse neighborhood of Klong Toey and started the Human Development Foundation for his poor neighbors of all religions. He holds advanced degrees in Theological Studies and Urban Planning as well as an honorary Doctorate in Social Administration from Thammasart University in Thailand. He is also the recipient of the Most Noble Order of the Crown of Thailand, The Koman Kim Tong Foundation Award, and the Bangkok Community Service Award for outstanding citizenship. Father Joe still lives in Klong Toey—in his Mercy Centre—where his work here first began.

For more information about the Human Development Foundation:
Phone: (662) 671-5313
Fax: (662) 671-7028
Email: info@mercycentre.org
Website: www.MercyCentre.org

   The foundation is always in great need of public and private donations, gifts, grants, and school and child sponsorships.